Debbie M

25 Years of Quilts

Dear Friends,

25 years, oh my!

How the years have flown and, goodness, how I have changed too! Feel free to laugh with me at this photo of me from around 1990. Hopefully, like our quilts, we're not getting older, we are getting better!! In fact, that is the concept for my 25th Anniversary book – to rediscover and update my favorite quilts from the last two and a half decades of design. Some quilt designs seem to stand the test of time, or, are just waiting to be given new life in updated colors and settings. From the hundreds of quilts I've designed for more than 55 quilt books, I've chosen twenty-five projects to refresh and reinterpret. To make these selections I scoured over thousands of pages of quilts and instructions. I looked for classic icons, a variety of techniques, easy to intermediate, and small to large quilt designs. Quilts that also topped the list are staff favorites and the quilts and themes that still "tickle me" after all this time. It was quite a trip down memory lane for me, recalling some of the trends that have come and gone and some that have come full circle. With each project I recount some of these memories as well as let you know why I selected certain quilts to reinvent. Redesigning these quilts really got my creative juices going, and challenged me to create new looks that made me as excited about the designs as I was the first time 'round.

Recycle, Refresh and Re-Interpret!

My Best,
Debbie

©2011 by Debbie Mumm • Leisure Arts, Inc., 5701 Ranch Drive, Little Rock, AR 72223 • www.leisurearts.com

TABLE OF Contents

Favorite Themes

4 Retro Hoot Owls
Wall Quilt

10 All the Buzz!
Wall Quilt

14 New Birds on the Block
Wall Quilt

20 Fashionista Scotties
Wall Quilt

24 Come Lately Ladybugs
Wall Art

28 Throw Me a Bone
Floor Quilt

33 Favorite Themes
Sampler Quilt

Pieced Beauties

40 New Memories
Metamorphosis Quilt

44 In the Jungle
Family Room Quilt

48 Wheels of Creativity
Lap Quilt

52 Random Red & White
Throw Quilt

Florals

56 Crazy Daisies
Throw Quilt

60 Friendly Daisies
Throw Quilt

65 Sunny Tulips
Bed Quilt

72 Fantasy Flowers
Bed Quilt

Fall Favorites

78 Colorful Fall Leaves
Wall Quilt

82 Happy Harvest
Wall Banner

87 Prairie Quail
Lap Quilt

Holiday Best

92 Happy Holidays Penguin
Wall Banner

97 Frosty & Friends
Wall Quilt

102 Greeter Santa
Door Banner

107 Santa Pockets
Card Holder

Unique Techniques

111 Sunflower Power
Dimensional Wall Quilt

116 French Linen Kitchen
Wall Art

120 Button Collection
Shadow Box

Et Cetera

1 About this Book

124 General Directions

128 About Debbie

128 Credits

Retro Hoot Owls

wall ▪ quilt

Retro Hoot Owls Wall Quilt Finished Size: 36" x 44½"	FIRST CUT		SECOND CUT	
	Number of Strips or Pieces	Dimensions	Number of Pieces	Dimensions
Fabric A Background ⅓ yard each of 4 Fabrics	1* 1* 1*	3½" x 42" 2½" x 42" 1½" x 42" *cut for each fabric	1* 1* 1* 2* 1* 2*	3½" x 19¾" 2½" x 16¾" 2½" x 12½" 2½" squares 1¾" x 10½" 1½" x 10½"
Fabric B Owl Head Obese Eighth each of 4 Fabrics	1* 2*	5½" x 10½" 1½" squares *cut for each fabric		
Fabric C Owl Body Fat Quarter each of 4 Fabrics	1*	10½" x 8½" *cut for each fabric		
Fabric D Branch Scrap each of 4 Fabrics	1*	1½" x 12½" *cut for each fabric		
First Border ⅙ yard	4	1" x 42"	2 2	1" x 40" 1" x 30½"
Second Border ⅙ yard	4	1" x 42"	2 2	1" x 41" 1" x 31½"
Outside Border ½ yard	5	2¼" x 42"	2	2¼" x 32½"
Binding ⅜ yard	5	2¼" x 42" ¼" finished binding		
Appliqués - Assorted scraps Backing - 1⅜ yards Batting - 40" x 49" Lightweight Fusible Web - ¾ yard				

Fabric Requirements and Cutting Instructions
Read all instructions before beginning and use ¼"-wide seam allowances throughout. Read Cutting Strips and Pieces on page 124 prior to cutting fabric.

Getting Started
These fanciful owls in their bright array of colors will be a delightful addition to any room. Block measures 15½" x 19¾" (unfinished). Refer to Accurate Seam Allowance on page 124. Whenever possible use Assembly Line Method on page 124. Press seams in direction of arrows.

Making the Block

1. Refer to Quick Corner Triangles on page 124. Making quick corner triangle units, sew two 1½" Fabric B squares to one 1½" x 10½" Fabric A piece as shown. Press.

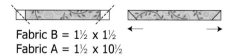

Fabric B = 1½ x 1½
Fabric A = 1½ x 10½

2. Sew unit from step 1 between one 1½" x 10½" Fabric A piece and one 5½" x 10½" Fabric B piece as shown. Press.

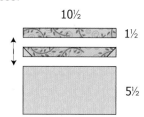

10½

1½

5½

Retro Hoot Owls Wall Quilt
36" x 44½"

5. Sew unit from step 2 to unit from step 4 as shown. Press.

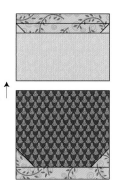

6. Sew unit from step 5 to one 2½" x 16¾" Fabric A strip as shown. Press.

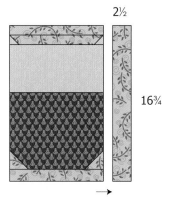

2½

16¾

7. Arrange and sew together unit from step 6, one 1½" x 12½" Fabric D piece, and one 2½" x 12½" Fabric A piece as shown. Press.

12½

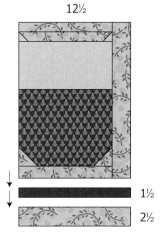

1½

2½

3. Making quick corner triangle units, sew two 2½" Fabric A squares to one 10½" x 8½" Fabric C piece as shown. Press.

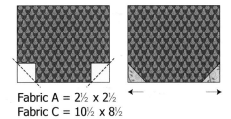

Fabric A = 2½ x 2½
Fabric C = 10½ x 8½

4. Sew unit from step 3 to one 1¾" x 10½" Fabric A piece as shown. Press.

10½

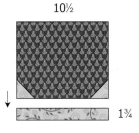

1¾

8. Sew one 3½" x 19¾" Fabric A strip to unit from step 7 as shown. Press. Block measures 15½" x 19¾"

3½

19¾

Block measures 15½" x 19¾"

9. Refer to steps 1-9 to make three additional blocks using different fabric combinations.

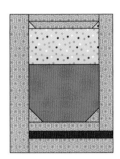

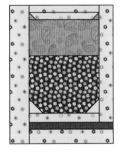

Adding the Appliqués
Refer to appliqué instructions on page 125. Our instructions use a combination of Quick-Fuse and Dimensional Appliqué. If you prefer hand appliqué, reverse patterns and add ¼"-wide seam allowances. Dimensional flower and centers will be added after quilting is complete. (Instructions on page 8.)

1. Use patterns on page 9 to trace large flower, flower center, owl eyes, beak, wings, and feet on paper side of fusible web. (Quantity needed noted on patterns.) Use appropriate fabrics to prepare all appliqués for fusing. Set flower center pieces aside until dimensional flowers are sewn to quilt.

It has been really fun to reinterpret my favorite themes and icons from my quilting history. However, I also wanted to include a new quilt with my newest favorite icon, the OWL! Like so many others, I am fascinated with retro trends from the 60's and 70's. For me the Owl is a playful part of the Mid Century kitsch look and makes me feel nostalgic for my youth. No matter what age we are now, the last owl trend was 40 to 50 years ago! I was 30 when I started my company. Gosh, I look like a kid in photos from the early days. I can't believe how quickly 25 years can fly by.

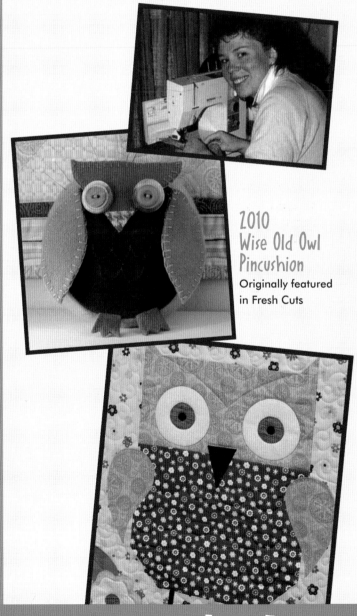

2010
Wise Old Owl
Pincushion
Originally featured in Fresh Cuts

2. Refer to photo on page 5 and layout on page 6 to position and fuse large flower and owl appliqués to blocks. Finish appliqué edges with machine satin stitch or other decorative stitching as desired.

Assembling and Adding the Borders

1. Arrange blocks into two rows with two blocks each. Sew blocks together. Press seams in opposite direction from row to row.

2. Sew rows together. Press.

3. Refer to Adding the Borders on page 126. Sew 1" x 30½" First Border strips to top and bottom of quilt. Press seams toward border. Sew two 1" x 40" First Border strips to sides. Press.

4. Sew 1" x 31½" Second Border strips to top and bottom of quilt. Press seams toward border just sewn. Sew two 1" x 41" Second Border strips to sides. Press.

5. Sew two 2¼" x 32½" Outside Border strips to top and bottom of quilt. Press seams toward border just sewn.

6. Sew 2¼" x 42" Outside Border strips together end-to-end to make one continuous 2¼"-wide Outside Border strip. Measure quilt through center from top to bottom including borders just added. Cut two 2¼"-wide Outside Border strips to this measurement. Sew to sides of quilt. Press.

Layering and Finishing

1. Referring to Layering the Quilt on page 126, arrange and baste backing, batting, and top together. Hand or machine quilt as desired.

2. Refer to Binding the Quilt on page 126. Sew 2¼" x 42" binding strips end-to-end to make one continuous 2¼"-wide binding strip. Bind quilt to finish. Note: Finished width of binding is ¼" instead of our normal ½".

3. Trace and cut a template using Dimensional Flower pattern on page 9.

4. Using dimensional flower template, trace pattern on wrong side of four pieces of fabric. Layer one marked fabric and one matching unmarked fabric right sides together.

5. Sew on traced line. Trim seams to ³⁄₁₆" and clip curves. Make a slit in the center of marked piece being careful not to cut other fabric. Turn right side out and press. Make four. Fuse flower center to dimensional piece. Make four.

6. Note: Dimensional flowers are attached to quilt when centers are sewn leaving flower edges free of stitches. Referring to photo on page 5 and layout on page 6, arrange and sew dimensional flowers to quilt centering them on large appliquéd flower shapes. Finish flower center edges with hand or machine decorative stitching as desired, stitching through all layers.

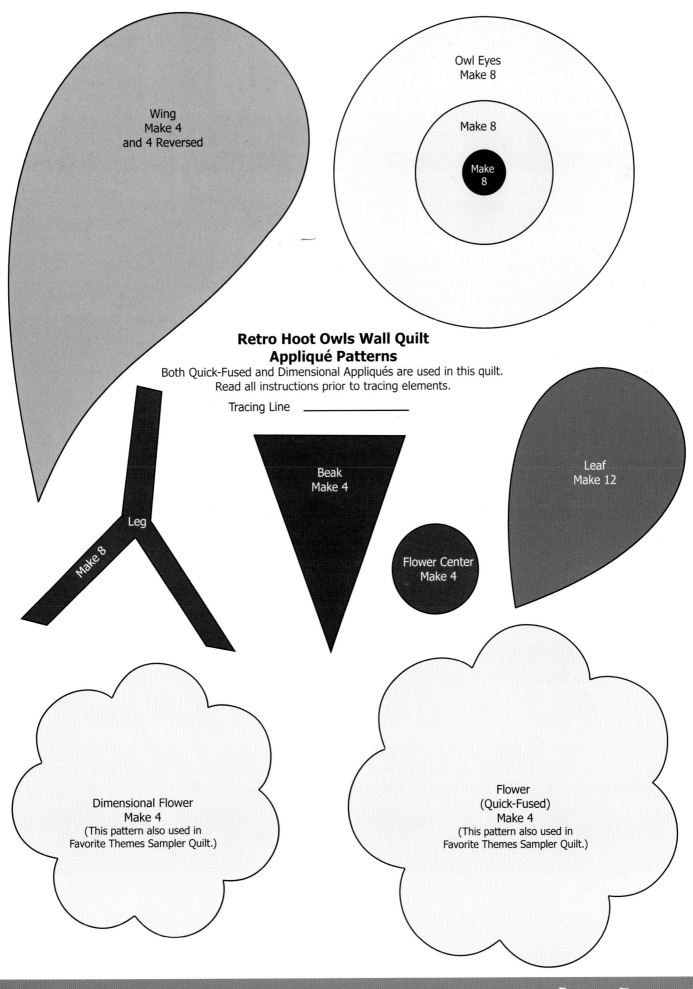

Wing
Make 4
and 4 Reversed

Owl Eyes
Make 8

Make 8

Make 8

Retro Hoot Owls Wall Quilt
Appliqué Patterns
Both Quick-Fused and Dimensional Appliqués are used in this quilt.
Read all instructions prior to tracing elements.

Tracing Line _____

Leg
Make 8

Beak
Make 4

Flower Center
Make 4

Leaf
Make 12

Dimensional Flower
Make 4
(This pattern also used in
Favorite Themes Sampler Quilt.)

Flower
(Quick-Fused)
Make 4
(This pattern also used in
Favorite Themes Sampler Quilt.)

All the Buzz!

wall ▪ quilt

All the Buzz! Wall Quilt Finished Size: 28½" x 28½"	FIRST CUT		SECOND CUT	
	Number of Strips or Pieces	Dimensions	Number of Pieces	Dimensions
Fabric A Background ⅓ yard	1	4½" x 42"	8	4½" squares
			1	2½" square
	1	1½" x 42"	4	1½" x 2½"
	2	1" x 42"	8	1" x 2½"
			8	1" x 2"
			8	1" x 1½"
			8	1" x 1"
Fabric B Lattice & Honeybee Heads ⅓ yard	1	1½" x 42"	4	1½" squares
	6	1" x 42"	2	1" x 26½"
			4	1" x 25½"
			2	1" x 12½"
			4	1" x 6½"
Fabric C Skep ⅓ yard	8	1" x 42"	16	1" x 6½"
			4	1" x 5½"
			4	1" x 4½"
			4	1" x 3½"
			32	1" x 3"
			4	1" x 2½"
Fabric D Skep Door scrap	4	1½" x 2½"		
Fabric E Skep Border ½ yard	2	6½" x 42"	4	6½" x 12½"
Outside Border ¼ yard	4	1¼" x 42"	2	1¼" x 28"
			2	1¼" x 26½"
Binding ⅜ yard	4	2¾" x 42"		
Appliqués - Assorted scraps Batting - 33" x 33" Ligthweight Fusible Web - ⅛ yard				

Fabric Requirements and Cutting Instructions

Read all instructions before beginning and use ¼"-wide seam allowances throughout. Read Cutting Strips and Pieces on page 124 prior to cutting fabric.

Getting Started

Bright shades of green against a field of brown give a graphic modern twist to a garden theme favorite. Skep Block measures 6½" square (unfinished) and Bee Block measures 12½" square (unfinished). Refer to Accurate Seam Allowance on page 124. Whenever possible use Assembly Line Method on page 124. Press seams in direction of arrows.

Making the Bee Block

1. Sew one 1½" x 2½" Fabric A piece between two 1½" Fabric B squares as shown. Press. Make two.

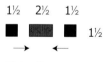

Make 2

2. Sew one 2½" Fabric A square between two 1½" x 2½" Fabric A pieces as shown. Press.

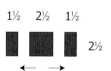

3. Sew one unit from step 2 between two units from step 1 as shown. Press.

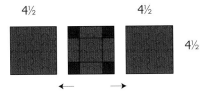

4. Sew unit from step 3 between two 4½" Fabric A squares. Press.

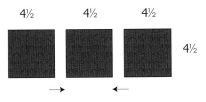

5. Sew three 4½" Fabric A squares together as shown. Press. Make two.

Make 2

6. Sew one unit from step 4 between two units from step 5 as shown. Press. Block measures 12½" square.

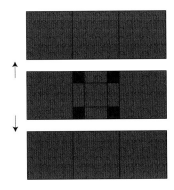

Block measures 12½"

Adding the Appliqués

Refer to appliqué instructions on page 125. Our instructions are for Quick-Fuse Appliqué, but if you prefer hand appliqué, reverse patterns and add ¼"-wide seam allowances.

1. Use patterns on pages 12 and 13 to trace four bee's bodies and eight wings on paper side of fusible web. Use appropriate fabrics to prepare all appliqués for fusing.

2. Refer to photo and layout on page 12 to position and fuse appliqués to block. Finish appliqué edges with machine satin stitch or other decorative stitching as desired.

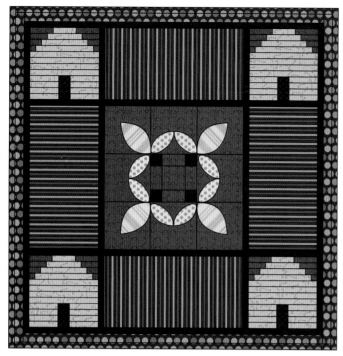

All the Buzz! Wall Quilt
28½" x 28½"

Making the Skep Blocks

1. Sew one 1" x 2½" Fabric C piece between two 1" x 2½" Fabric A pieces as shown. Press. Make four.

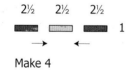

Make 4

2. Sew one 1" x 3½" Fabric C piece between two 1" x 2" Fabric A pieces as shown. Press. Make four.

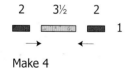

Make 4

3. Sew one 1" x 4½" Fabric C piece between two 1" x 1½" Fabric A pieces as shown. Press. Make four.

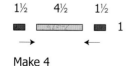

Make 4

All the Buzz! Wall Quilt
Patterns are reversed for use with Quick-Fuse Appliqué (page 125)

Tracing Line _____

4. Sew one 1" x 5½" Fabric C piece between two 1" Fabric A squares as shown. Press. Make four. Arrange and sew together units from steps 1-4 as shown. Press. Make four.

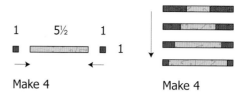

Make 4   Make 4

5. Sew four 1" x 6½" Fabric C pieces together as shown. Press. Make four.

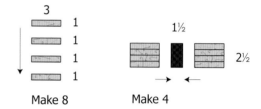

Make 4

6. Sew four 1" x 3" Fabric C pieces together as shown. Press. Make eight. Sew one 1½" x 2½" Fabric D piece between two of these units. Press. Make four.

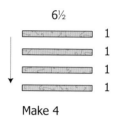

Make 8   Make 4

7. Arrange and sew together one unit from step 4, one unit from step 5 and one unit from step 6 as shown. Press. Make four. Block measures 6½" square.

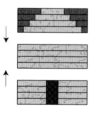

Make 4
Block measures 6½"

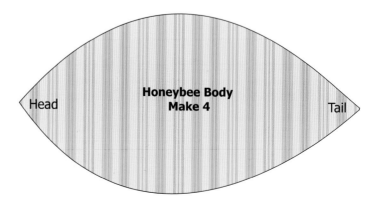

Head   **Honeybee Body**
Make 4   Tail

1995 Homeward Bound
Originally featured in Angel Wings & Growing Things

1999 Honey Bee Table Quilt
Originally featured in Cottage in Bloom

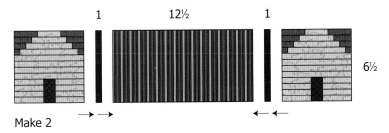

In our backyards, it's kind of a love~hate relationship that we have with bees. But in our arts and crafts world, we do love our bees! Whether it's a chubby bumble bee, a friendly honeybee or ladies gathering at a quilting bee – the bee continues to "bee" a favorite icon in the quilting culture. I combined elements from two previous projects to create this updated version with dots, stripes and swirled fabrics. The pieced honeybees originally appeared in the 1999 Honey Bee Table Quilt from the book Cottage in Bloom and the beehives go back to 1995 from the book Angel Wings & Growing Things. By the way – one of my favorite book titles ever. I love to say it – it just rolls off your tongue.

Assembling, Layering and Finishing

1. Arrange and sew together two Skep blocks, two 1" x 6½" Fabric B pieces, and one 6½" x 12½" Fabric E piece as shown. Press. Make two.

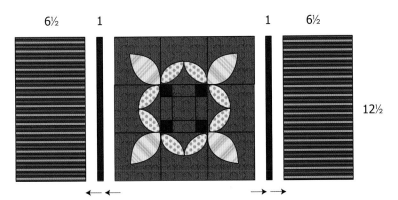

Make 2

2. Arrange and sew together two 6½" x 12½" Fabric E pieces, two 1" x 12½" Fabric B pieces, and Bee block as shown. Press.

3. Referring to photo on page 11 and layout on page 12, arrange and sew together four 1" x 25½" Fabric B strips and rows from step 1 and 2. Press. Sew two 1" x 26½" Fabric B strips to sides of quilt. Press.

4. Sew two 1¼" x 26½" Outside Border strips to top and bottom of quilt. Press. Sew two 1¼" x 28" Outside Border strips to sides of quilt. Press.

5. Referring to Layering the Quilt on page 126, arrange and baste backing, batting, and top together. Hand or machine quilt as desired.

6. Refer to Binding the Quilt on page 126. Use 2¾"-wide binding strips to bind quilt.

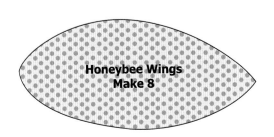

Honeybee Wings
Make 8

New Birds on the Block
wall ■ quilt

New Birds on the Block Wall Quilt Finished Size: 67½" x 47½"	FIRST CUT		SECOND CUT	
	Number of Strips or Pieces	Dimensions	Number of Pieces	Dimensions
Fabric A Block Accent ¼ yard	2	3" x 42"	24	3" squares
Fabric B Triangles 1 yard	10	3" x 42"	24 72	3" x 5½" 3" squares
Fabric C Block Background 1 yard	6	5½" x 42"	24 24	5½" squares 5½" x 3"
Fabric D Bird Background 1 yard	3 2 3	5½" x 42" 3" x 42" 2½" x 42"	6 12 24 24 24	5½" x 9½" 5½" x 2½" 3" squares 2½" squares 2½" x 2"
Fabric E Quilt Background ⅞ yard	9	3" x 42"	24 24	3" x 8" 3" x 5½"
Fabric F Block Accent ½ yard	7	2" x 42"	24 48	2" x 5½" 2" squares
First Border ¼ yard	5	1" x 42"		
Second Border ⅓ yard	6	1¼" x 42"		
Outside Border ½ yard	6	2½" x 42"		
Binding ⅝ yard	7	2¾" x 42"		

Appliqués - Assorted scraps
Backing - 3⅛ yards
Batting - 75" x 55"
Lightweight Fusible Web - ½ yard
⅛" Buttons - 6 for eyes

Fabric Requirements and Cutting Instructions
Read all instructions before beginning and use ¼"-wide seam allowances throughout. Read Cutting Strips and Pieces on page 124 prior to cutting fabric.

Getting Started
Bring Spring into your home with this easy-to-make six-block quilt featuring a delightful and colorful flock of birds. Block measures 20½" square (unfinished). Refer to Accurate Seam Allowance on page 124. Whenever possible use Assembly Line Method on page 124. Press seams in direction of arrows.

Making the Blocks

1. Sew one 3" Fabric A square to one 3" Fabric B square as shown. Press. Make twenty-four, twelve of each variation. Sew one 3" x 5½" Fabric B piece to unit as shown. Press. Make twenty-four, twelve of each variation.

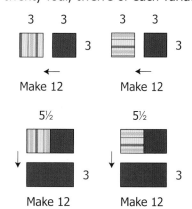

New Birds on the Block Wall Quilt
67½" x 47½"

2. Refer to Quick Corner Triangles on page 125. Making a quick corner triangle unit, sew one 5½" Fabric C to one unit from step 1 as shown. Press. Make twenty-four, twelve of each variation.

C = 5½ x 5½
Unit from step 1
Make 24
(12 of each variation)

3. Making a quick-corner triangle unit, sew one 2½" Fabric D square to one unit from step 2 as shown. Press. Make twenty-four, twelve of each variation.

D = 2½ x 2½
Unit from step 2
Make 24
(12 of each variation)

4. Making a quick corner triangle unit, sew one 3" Fabric D square to one 3" x 8" Fabric E piece as shown. Press. Make twenty-four. Press twelve as shown and twelve in opposite direction.

Fabric D = 3 x 3
Fabric E = 3 x 8
Make 24
(Press 12 in opposite direction.)

5. Sew one 3" x 5½" Fabric E piece to one unit from step 3 as shown. Press. Sew one unit from step 4 to unit from this step as shown. Press. Make twenty-four, twelve of each variation.

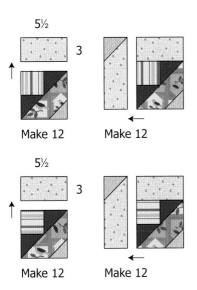

Make 12   Make 12

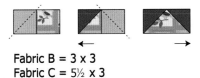

Make 12   Make 12

6. Making quick corner triangle units, sew two 3" Fabric B squares to one 5½" x 3" Fabric C piece as shown. Press. Make twenty-four.

Fabric B = 3 x 3
Fabric C = 5½ x 3
Make 24

7. Sew one 2½"x 2" Fabric D piece between two 2" Fabric F squares as shown. Press. Make twenty-four.

2   2½   2

2

Make 24

8. Sew one 2" x 5½" Fabric F piece between one unit from step 6 and one unit from step 7 as shown. Press. Make twenty-four.

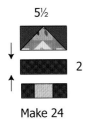

5½

2

Make 24

This project really showcases how you can entirely change the look and feel of a quilt by the colors and fabrics you choose. The dark, deep colors of this original lodge-style quilt were very popular in the early 2000's when I designed Forest Friends for our book, Cozy Northwest Christmas (circa 2003). In addition, I changed the center icon to birds and simplified the border. You can swap and resize appliqué icons from one project and put them in another to customize projects to your personal taste and preferences. Isn't that the fun of creating your own projects!

2003
Forest Friends
Originally featured in Cozy Northwest Christmas

9. Sew one 5½" x 2½" Fabric D piece to one unit from step 8 as shown. Press. Make twelve. Sew this unit between two units from step 5 as shown. Press. Make twelve, press six as shown and six in opposite direction.

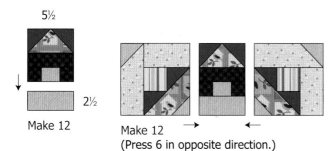

5½

2½

Make 12

Make 12
(Press 6 in opposite direction.)

10. Sew one 5½" x 9½" Fabric D piece between two units from step 8 as shown. Press. Make six.

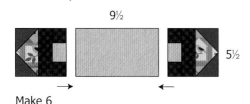

9½

5½

Make 6

11. Sew one unit from step 10 between two units from step 9 as shown. Press. Make six, press three as shown and three in opposite direction. Block measures 20½" square.

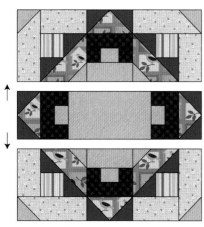

Make 6
(Press 3 in opposite direction.)
Block measures 20½"

Adding the Appliqués

Refer to appliqué instructions on page 125. Our instructions are for Quick-Fuse Appliqué, but if you prefer hand appliqué, reverse patterns and add ¼"-wide seam allowances.

1. Use pattern on page 19 to trace six birds on paper side of fusible web, three of each variation. Use appropriate fabrics to prepare all appliqués for fusing.

2. Refer to photo on page 15 and layout on page 16 to position and fuse appliqués to each block. Finish appliqué edges with machine satin stitch or other decorative stitching as desired. Add buttons for eyes after quilting.

Assembling and Adding the Borders

1. Refer to photo on page 15 and layout on page 16 to sew two rows of three blocks each. Press seams in opposite direction from row to row.

2. Sew rows together. Press.

3. Refer to Adding the Borders on page 126. Measure quilt through center from side to side. Cut two 1"-wide First Border strips to this measurement. Sew to top and bottom of quilt. Press seams toward border.

4. Sew 1" x 42" First Border strips together end-to-end to make one continuous 1"-wide First Border strip. Measure quilt through center from top to bottom including borders just added. Cut two 1"-wide First Border strips to this measurement. Sew to sides of quilt. Press.

5. Refer to steps 1 and 2 to join, measure, trim, and sew 1¼"-wide Second Border, and 2½"-wide Outside Border strips to top, bottom, and sides of quilt. Press.

Layering and Finishing

1. Cut backing crosswise into two equal pieces. Sew pieces together lengthwise to make one 80" x 55" (approximate) backing piece. Press.

2. Referring to Layering the Quilt on page 126, arrange and baste backing, batting, and top together. Hand or machine quilt as desired.

3. Refer to Binding the Quilt on page 126. Sew 2¾" x 42" binding strips end-to-end to make one continuous 2¾"-wide binding strip. Bind quilt to finish.

New Birds on the Block Wall Quilt

Tracing Line _____
Tracing Line - - - - - - - - - - - - - - - -
(will be hidden behind other fabrics)

Make 3

Make 3

Fashionista Scotties

wall ■ quilt

Fashionista Scotties Wall Quilt Finished Size: 38½" x 40½"	FIRST CUT		SECOND CUT	
	Number of Strips or Pieces	Dimensions	Number of Pieces	Dimensions
Fabric A Background ¾ yard	14	1½" x 42"	2 5 8 12 24 24 48	1½" x 33½" 1½" x 29½" 1½" x 7½" 1½" x 6½" 1½" x 3½" 1½" x 2½" 1½" squares
Fabric B Scottie Dog ⅓ yard each of 3 Fabrics	1* 1* 2*	3½" x 42" 2½" x 42" 1½" x 42" *cut for each fabric	4* 4* 8* 16*	3½" x 9½" 2½" x 6½" 1½" x 3½" 1½" squares
Fabric C Accent Border ⅙ yard	4	1" x 42"	2 2	1" x 33½" 1" x 31½"
First Border ⅙ yard	4	1" x 42"	2 2	1" x 34½" 1" x 31½"
Second Border ¼ yard	4	1¼" x 42"	2 2	1¼" x 36" 1¼" x 32½"
Outside Border ⅓ yard	4	2½" x 42"	2 2	2½" x 40" 2½" x 34"
Binding ⅜ yard	4	2¾" x 42"		

Scarf Appliqués - Assorted scraps
Backing - 1¼ yards (Fabric needs to be at least 45"-wide.)
Batting - 43" x 45"
Lightweight Fusible Web - ⅓ yard
Assorted Buttons - 12 for eyes
Assorted Buttons or Brooches - 12 for Scarves

Fabric Requirements and Cutting Instructions

Read all instructions before beginning and use ¼"-wide seam allowances throughout. Read Cutting Strips and Pieces on page 124 prior to cutting fabric.

Getting Started

Have fun dressing these stylish dogs in colorful neckerchiefs and lots of bling! Block measures 9½" x 7½" (unfinished). Refer to Accurate Seam Allowance on page 124. Whenever possible use Assembly Line Method on page 124. Press seams in direction of arrows.

Making the Blocks

1. Refer to Quick Corner Triangles on page 124. Making a quick corner triangle unit, sew one 1½" Fabric B square to one 1½" x 6½" Fabric A piece as shown. Press. Make four.

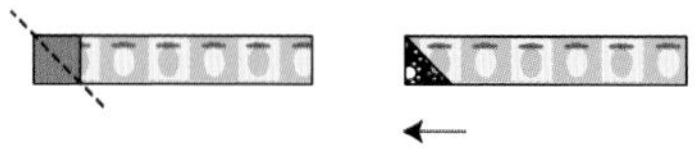

Fabric B = 1½ x 1½
Fabric A = 1½ x 6½
Make 4

2. Making a quick corner triangle unit, sew one 1½" Fabric B square to one 1½" x 3½" Fabric A piece as shown. Press. Make four.

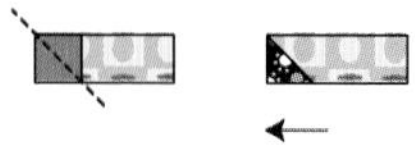

Fabric B = 1½ x 1½
Fabric A = 1½ x 3½
Make 4

3. Sew one unit from step 1 to one unit from step 2 as shown. Press. Make four.

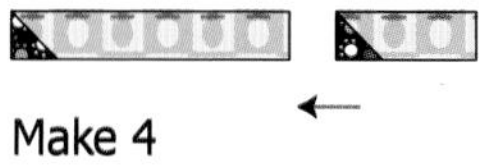

Make 4

4. Making quick corner triangle unit, sew one 1½" Fabric B square to one 1½" x 2½" Fabric A piece as shown. Press. Make four. Sew one 1½" Fabric B square to one 1½" Fabric A square as shown. Press. Make four.

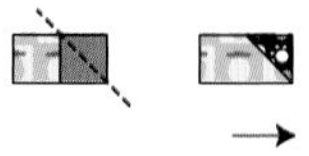

Fabric B = 1½ x 1½
Fabric A = 1½ x 2½
Make 4

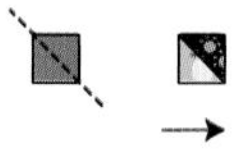

Fabric B = 1½ x 1½
Fabric A = 1½ x 1½
Make 4

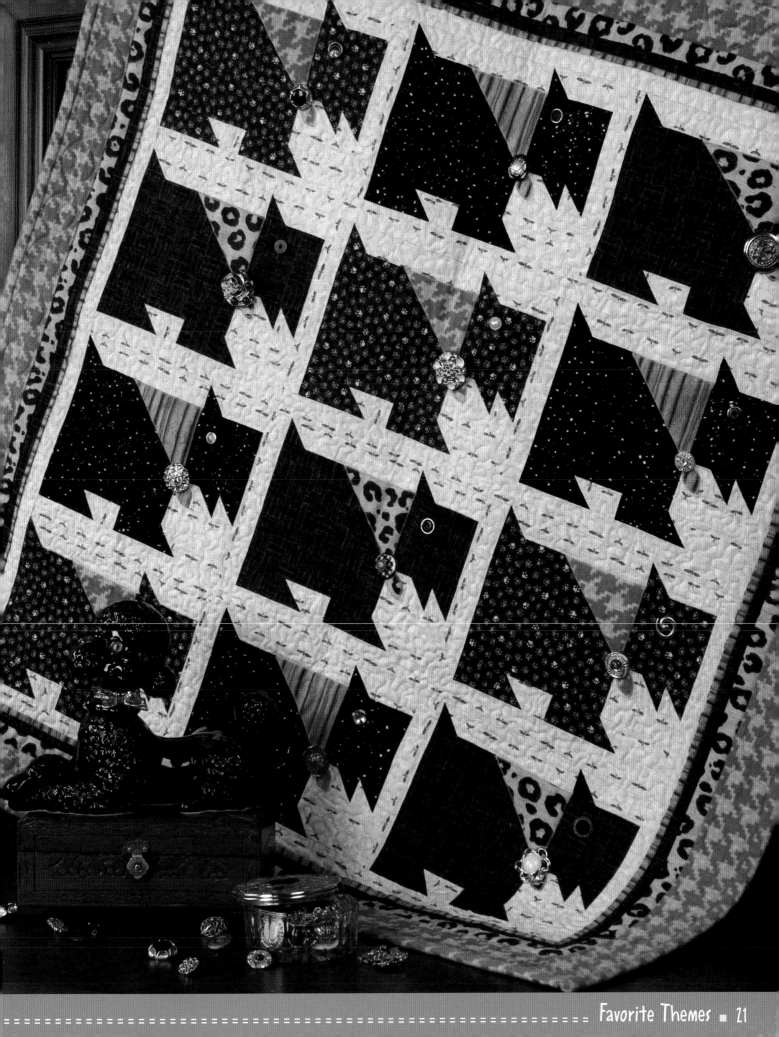

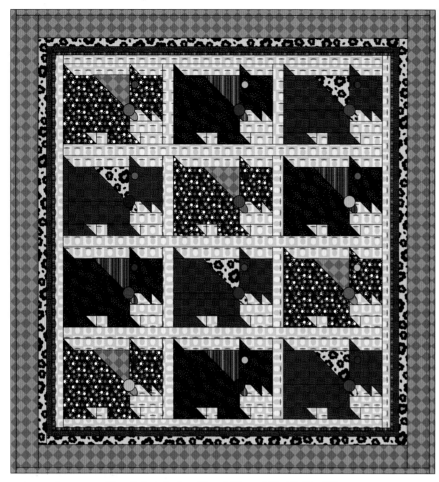

Fashionista Scotties Wall Quilt
38½" x 40½"

7. Making a quick corner triangle unit, sew one 1½" Fabric A square to one 1½" x 3½" Fabric B piece as shown. Press. Make eight.

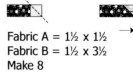

Fabric A = 1½ x 1½
Fabric B = 1½ x 3½
Make 8

8. Arrange and sew together two units from step 7, one 1½" Fabric A square, and one 1½" x 2½" Fabric A piece as shown. Press. Make four.

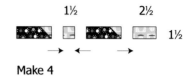

Make 4

9. Arrange and sew together one unit from step 3, one 3½" x 9½" Fabric B piece, one unit from step 6, and one unit from step 8 as shown. Press. Make four. Block measures 9½" x 7½".

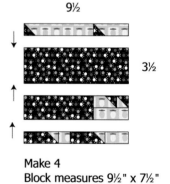

Make 4
Block measures 9½" x 7½"

5. Sew two units from step 4, one of each variation, together as shown. Press. Make four. Sew this unit to one 1½" x 3½" Fabric A piece. Press. Make four.

Make 4

Make 4

6. Sew one 2½" x 6½" Fabric B piece to one unit from step 5 as shown. Press. Make four.

Make 4

10. Referring to steps 1-10 to make eight more blocks, four of each Fabric B combination.

Make 4   Make 4

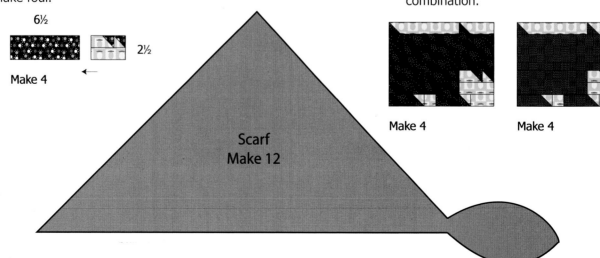

Scarf
Make 12

1992
Scotties on Parade
Originally featured in
More Quick Country Quilting

These Scotties had a mini-make-over before they paraded around town again. Naturally, the first time 'round I dressed these pups up in the traditional red and black color scheme that we associate with Scotty dogs. For their modern make-over, I chose more trendy color accents to accompany their black fur bodies. Hearts were one of my favorite background quilting themes at the time (1992), but I replaced the hearts with a less sentimental zig-zag pattern of quilting to mimic the dogs' long furry locks. The scarves are now a bit jauntier and less shawl-like. Little changes can make a big difference!

Adding the Appliqués

Refer to appliqué instructions on page 125. Our instructions are for Quick-Fuse Appliqué, but if you prefer hand appliqué, add ¼"-wide seam allowances.

1. Use pattern on page 22 to trace twelve scarves on paper side of fusible web. Use appropriate fabrics to prepare all appliqués for fusing.

2. Refer to photo on page 21 and layout on page 22 to position and fuse appliqués to block. Finish appliqué edges with machine satin stitch or other decorative stitching as desired.

Assembling the Quilt

1. Sew three blocks and two 1½" x 7½" Fabric A strips together as shown. Press. Make four rows referring to photo on page 21 and layout on page 22 for block placement.

1½   1½

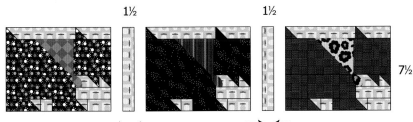

7½

Make 4 Rows
(in assorted block combinations)

2. Referring to photo on page 21 and layout on page 22, arrange and sew together five 1½" x 29½" Fabric A strips and rows from step 1. Press.

3. Sew two 1½" x 33½" Fabric A strips to sides of quilt. Press.

Adding the Borders

1. Fold one 1" x 31½" Fabric C strip in half lengthwise wrong sides together to make a ½" x 31½" folded piece. Press. Make two. Place two folded strips on quilt (top and bottom) with raw edges matching and folded edge in toward center. Stay-stitch in place. Repeat step to fold, align and stay stitch two 1" x 33½" Fabric C strips to sides of quilt.

2. Sew two 1" x 31½" First Border strips to top and bottom of quilt. Press seams toward border. Sew two 1" x 34½" First Border strips to sides of quilt. Press.

3. Sew two 1¼" x 32½" Second Border strips to top and bottom of quilt. Press seams toward border just sewn. Sew two 1¼" x 36" Second Border strips to sides of quilt. Press.

4. Sew two 2½" x 34" Outside Border strips to top and bottom of quilt. Press seams toward border just sewn. Sew two 2½" x 40" Outside Border strips to sides of quilt. Press.

Layering and Finishing

1. Referring to Layering the Quilt on page 126, arrange and baste backing, batting, and top together. Hand or machine quilt as desired.

2. Refer to Binding the Quilt on page 126. Use 2¾"-wide binding strips to bind quilt. Referring to photo on page 21, sew assorted buttons and brooches to quilt.

Come Lately Ladybugs
wall ∎ art

Come Lately Ladybugs Wall Art Finished Size: 20" x 20" over stretcher bars	FIRST CUT		SECOND CUT	
	Number of Strips or Pieces	Dimensions	Number of Pieces	Dimensions
Fabric A Background scrap each of 4 Fabrics	1*	6½" square *cut for each fabric		
Fabric B Border Center Block ⅛ yard	1	1½" x 42"	20	1½" squares
Fabric C Block Border Light ⅓ yard	1 1 2	3½" x 42" 2½" x 42" 1" x 42"	20 20 20 20	3½" x 1" 2½" x 1" 1" x 2½" 1" x 1½"
Fabric D Block Border Dark ¼ yard	6	1" x 42"	20 40 20	1" x 3½" 1" x 2½" 1" x 1½"
Outside Border ½ yard	3	4" x 42"	2 2	4" x 25½" 4" x 18½"
Appliqués - Assorted scraps Backing - ⅞ yard Batting - 30" x 30" Lightweight Fusible Web - ¼ yard Four 20" Stretcher Bars Staple Gun & Staples Picture or Sawtooth Hanger				

Fabric Requirements and Cutting Instructions
Read all instructions before beginning and use ¼"-wide seam allowances throughout. Read Cutting Strips and Pieces on page 124 prior to cutting fabric.

Getting Started
Ladybugs go modern on this contemporary wall art. The quilt is wrapped around stretcher bars for a decorative - friendly presentation. Border block measures 3½" square (unfinished). Refer to Accurate Seam Allowance on page 124. Whenever possible use Assembly Line Method on page 124. Press seams in direction of arrows.

Making the Quilt

1. Sew two different 6½" Fabric A squares together as shown. Press. Make two noting pressing arrow direction.

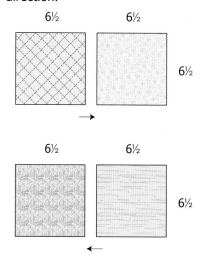

2. Sew units from step 1 together as shown. Press.

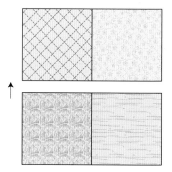

3. Sew one 1½" Fabric B square between two 1" x 1½" Fabric D pieces. Press. Sew this unit between two 1" x 2½" Fabric D pieces as shown. Press. Make ten.

1   1

 2½

← →

Make 10

5. Sew one 1½" Fabric B square between two 1" x 1½" Fabric C pieces. Press. Sew this unit between two 2½" x 1" Fabric C pieces as shown. Press. Make ten.

1   1

2½

← →

Make 10

4. Sew one unit from step 3 between two 1" x 2½" Fabric C pieces. Press. Sew this unit between two 3½" x 1" Fabric C pieces as shown. Press. Make ten.

1   1

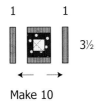 3½

← →

Make 10

6. Sew one unit from step 5 between two 1" x 2½" Fabric D pieces. Press. Sew this unit between two 1" x 3½" Fabric D pieces as shown. Press. Make ten.

1   1

 3½

→   ←

Make 10

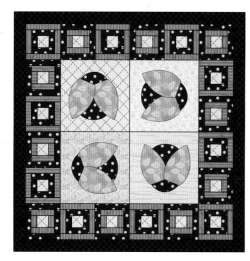

Come Lately Ladybugs Wall Art
20" x 20"

9. Sew two 4" x 18½" Outside Border strips to top and bottom of quilt. Press seams toward border just sewn.

10. Sew two 4" x 25½" Outside Border strips to sides of quilt. Press.

Adding the Appliqués
Refer to appliqué instructions on page 125. Our instructions are for Quick-Fuse Appliqué, but if you prefer hand appliqué, reverse patterns and add ¼"-wide seam allowances.

1. Use pattern below to trace four ladybugs on paper side of fusible web. Use appropriate fabrics to prepare all appliqués for fusing.

2. Refer to photo on page 25 and layout to position and fuse appliqués to quilt. Finish appliqué edges with machine satin stitch or other decorative stitching as desired.

Finishing the Wall Art

1. Referring to Layering the Quilt on page 126, arrange and baste backing, batting, and top together. Hand or machine quilt as desired. Trim backing and batting to match quilt.

7. Arrange and sew together two units from step 6 and two units from step 4 alternating units as shown. Press. Make two. Sew to top and bottom of unit from step 2. Press.

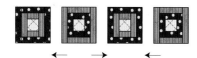

Make 2

8. Arrange and sew together three units from step 4 and three units from step 6 alternating units as shown. Press. Make two. Sew to sides of unit from step 7.

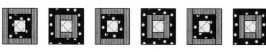

Make 2

Come Lately Ladybugs Wall Art
Patterns are reversed for use with Quick-Fuse Appliqué (page 125)

Tracing Line ——————
Tracing Line - - - - - - - - - - - -
(will be hidden behind other fabrics)

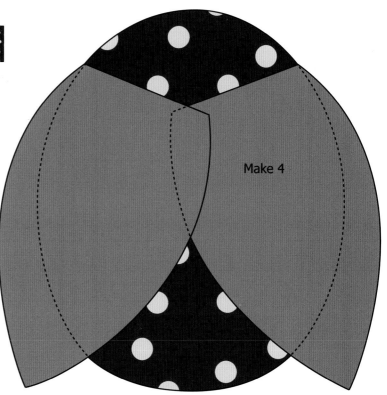

Make 4

2. If using interlocking stretcher bars, slide four 20" bars together. Check for square by measuring from corner to corner. Staple at corners. (Note: A 20" square canvas frame can be used instead.)

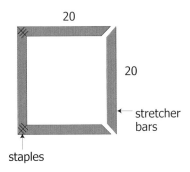

20

20

stretcher bars

staples

3. Stretch quilt around frame, staple in the middle on each side pulling fabric tightly to obtain good tension. Turn piece over to check block placement and adjust as needed. Continue process, working from center, stretching and stapling fabric, stopping at corners.

Back View

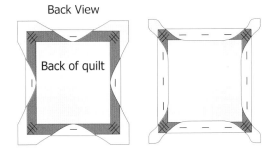

Back of quilt

4. Pull corner tight and check front to make sure quilt is taut. Fold excess fabric at 90°, crease, and form corner. Staple tightly to back.

5. Attach a wire picture hanger or sawtooth hanger to back of wall piece.

I've been fond of ladybugs since the early 60's when I wore two tiny red ladybug pins on the lapel of my coat. The first time 'round on this project, I took it in a more whimsical direction. This version is still playful, but by narrowing the color story to basically two on-trend colors, it looks more contemporary and is more apt to fit into home color schemes. When designs are simplified and more graphic like this new interpretation of ladybugs, they have a more modern, decorative look which makes them perfect for wall art. By wrapping the quilted design around stretcher bars, it solidifies the decorative quality of the project.

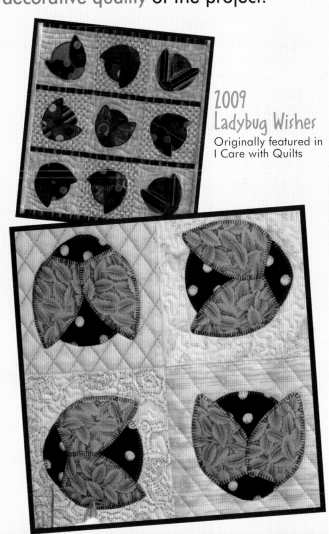

2009 Ladybug Wishes
Originally featured in I Care with Quilts

Throw Me a Bone

floor ▪ quilt

Throw Me a Bone Floor Quilt Finished Size: 42" x 59"	FIRST CUT		SECOND CUT	
	Number of Strips or Pieces	Dimensions	Number of Pieces	Dimensions
Fabric A Paw Background, Block 1 Border & Block 2 Center 1 yard	1 3 6	6½" x 42" 3½" x 42" 2½" x 42"	3 24 6 6	6½" squares 3½" squares 2½" x 17½" 2½" x 13½"
Fabric B Block 1 Center & Block 2 Border ⅔ yard	1 6	6½" x 42" 2½" x 42"	3 6 6	6½" squares 2½" x 17½" 2½" x 13½"
Fabric C Bone Background ½ yard	4	3½" x 42"	24	3½" x 6½"
Fabric D Block Accent Squares ¼ yard	3	2" x 42"	48	2" squares
Fabric E Block Accent Borders ½ yard	13	1" x 42"	10 12 12	1" x 17½" 1" x 13½" 1" x 12½"
Outside Border ⅔ yard	1 5	4½" x 42" 3½" x 42"	4 10	4½" squares 3½" x 17½"
Binding ⅝ yard	6	2¾" x 42"		
Paw Appliqués - ⅛ yard Bone Appliqués - ¼ yard Backing - 2⅔ yards Batting - 48" x 65" Lightweight Fusible Web - ¾ yard				

Fabric Requirements and Cutting Instructions Read all instructions before beginning and use ¼"-wide seam allowances throughout. Read Cutting Strips and Pieces on page 124 prior to cutting fabric.

Getting Started Pamper your pet by making this easy to construct quilt with simple fused appliqués. Block measures 17½" square (unfinished). Refer to Accurate Seam Allowance on page 124. Whenever possible use Assembly Line Method on page 124. Press seams in direction of arrows.

Making the Blocks

1. Sew one 3½" x 6 ½" Fabric C piece between two 3½" Fabric A squares as shown. Press. Make twelve.

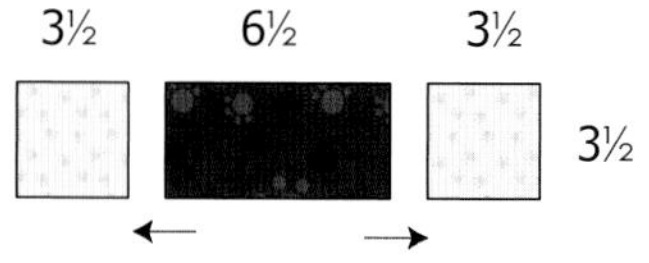

Make 12

2. Sew one 6½" Fabric B square between two 3½" x 6½" Fabric C pieces as shown. Press. Make three of Unit 1. Sew one 6½" Fabric A square between two 3½" x 6½" Fabric C pieces as shown. Press. Make three of Unit 2.

Unit 1

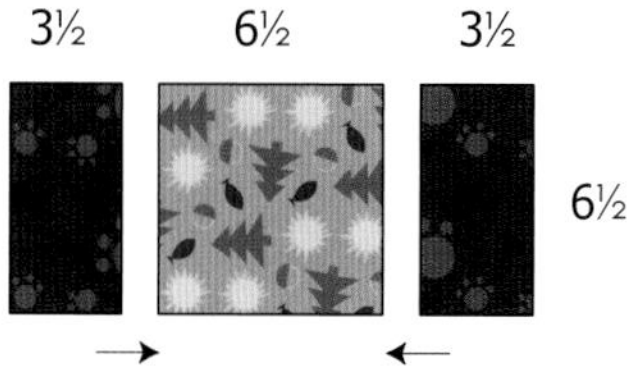

Make 3

Unit 2

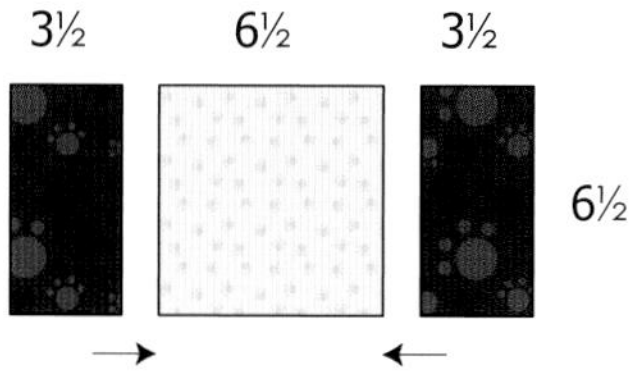

Make 3

Throw Me a Bone Floor Quilt
42" x 59"

4. Sew one unit from step 3 between two 1" x 12½" Fabric E strips. Press seams toward Fabric E. Sew this unit between two 1" x 13½" Fabric E strips as shown. Press. Make six, three of Unit 1 and three of Unit 2.

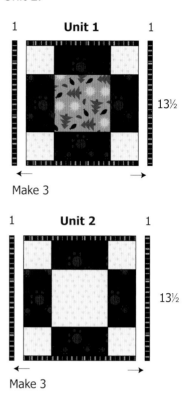

3. Sew one unit from step 2 between two units from step 1 as shown. Press. Make six, three of Unit 1 and three of Unit 2.

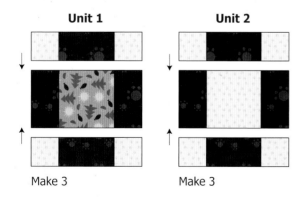

5. Sew one Unit 1 from step 4 between two 2½" x 13½" Fabric A strips. Press seams toward Fabric A. Sew this unit between two 2½" x 17½" Fabric A strips as shown. Press. Make three.

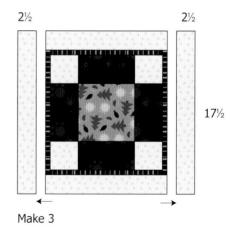

1996
Regal Beagles
Originally featured in
Bowsers & Meowsers

Since becoming a Dog Grandma recently, I have noticed even more keenly just how many dog lovers there are out there. We've made quite a few pet quilts over the years and particularly for our 1996 book entitled "Bowsers and Meowsers." I realize I took quite a bit of license with the English language for that title, but it was certainly playful. When it comes to designing fabric, I receive lots of requests for bones and paws since they go with every breed of dog. The simple piecing and appliqués make it easy to sew up this floor quilt for the family pup.

6. Refer to Quick Corner Triangles on page 124. Making quick corner triangle units, sew four 2" Fabric D squares to one unit from step 5 as shown. Press. Make three and label Block 1. Block measures 17½" square.

Block 1

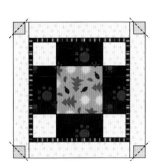
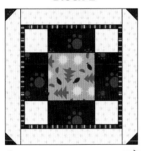

Fabric D = 2 x 2
Unit from step 5
Make 3

Block measures 17½" square

7. Sew one Unit 2 from step 4 between two 2½" x 13½" Fabric B strips. Press seams toward Fabric B. Sew this unit between two 2½" x 17½" Fabric B strips as shown. Press. Make three.

2½   2½

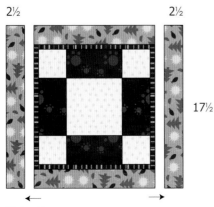

17½

Make 3

8. Making quick corner triangle units, sew four 2" Fabric D squares to one unit from step 7 as shown. Press. Make three and label Block 2. Block measures 17½" square.

Block 2

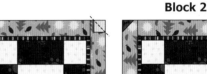

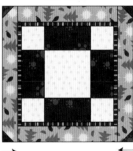

Fabric D = 2 x 2
Unit from step 7
Make 3

Block measures 17½" square

Adding the Appliqués
Refer to appliqué instructions on page 125. Our instructions are for Quick-Fuse Appliqué, but if you prefer hand appliqué, add ¼"-wide seam allowances.

1. Use patterns on page 32 to trace twelve paws and twelve bones on paper side of fusible web. Use appropriate fabrics to prepare all appliqués for fusing.

2. Refer to photo on page 29 and layout on page 30 to position and fuse four bones and four paws to each block. Finish appliqué edges with machine satin stitch or other decorative stitching as desired.

Assembling and Adding the Borders

1. Referring to photo on page 29 and layout on page 30 arrange and sew together three rows each with one Block 1 and one Block 2. Press seams in opposite direction from row to row. Sew rows together. Press.

2. Draw a diagonal line on wrong side of one 4½" Outside Border square. Place marked square and one 4½" Outside Border square right sides together. (Note: When using directional fabric, both squares must face in the same direction.) Sew scant ¼" away from drawn line on both sides to make half-square triangles as shown. Make two. Cut on drawn line and press. Square to 4". This will make four half-square triangle units.

Outside Border = 4½ x 4½
Make 2

Square to 4"
Make 4
Half-square Triangles Units

3. Refer to diagram below to determine which corner Fabric D is sewn to. Refer to Quick Corner Triangles on page 124. Making a quick corner triangle unit, sew one 2" Fabric D square to unit from step 2 as shown. Press. Make four.

Unit from step 2
Fabric D = 2 x 2
Make 4

4. Sew one 3½" x 17½" Outside Border strip to one 1" x 17½" Fabric E strip. Press. Make ten.

5. Refer to Quick Corner Triangles on page 124. Making quick corner triangle units, sew two 2" Fabric D squares to one unit from step 4 as shown. Press. Make ten.

Unit from step 4
Fabric D = 2 x 2
Make 10

6. Referring to photo on page 29 and layout on page 30, arrange and sew together two units from step 5. Press. Make two and sew to top and bottom of quilt. Press.

7. Referring to photo on page 29 and layout on page 30, arrange and sew together two units from step 3 and three units from step 5. Press. Make two and sew to sides of quilt.

Layering and Finishing

1. Cut backing crosswise into two equal pieces. Sew pieces together lengthwise to make one 48" x 80" (approximate) backing piece. Press and trim to 48" x 65".

2. Referring to Layering the Quilt on page 126, arrange and baste backing, batting, and top together. Hand or machine quilt as desired.

3. Refer to Binding the Quilt on page 126. Use 2¾"-wide binding strips to bind quilt.

**Throw Me a Bone
Floor Quilt**
Patterns are reversed for use with
Quick-Fuse Appliqué (page 125)

Tracing Line _____

Paw
Make 24

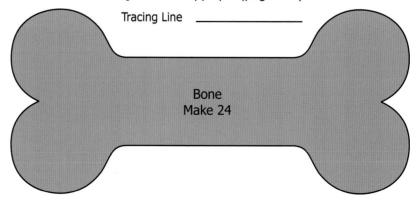

Bone
Make 24

Favorite Themes
sampler ▪ quilt

Favorite Themes Sampler Quilt Finished Size: 33" x 31½"	FIRST CUT	
	Number of Strips or Pieces	Dimensions
Owl Block		
Fabric A Background ⅛ yard or ⅓ yard directional each of 3 Fabrics	2* 2* 2*	10" x 1¾" 2" x 5½" 1½" squares *cut for each fabric (adjust cuts for directional fabric)
Fabric B Owl Face & Ears Scrap each of 3 Fabrics	1* 2*	3" x 5½" 1¼" squares *cut for each fabric
Fabric C Owl Body Scrap each of 3 Fabrics	1*	5½" x 4½" *cut for each fabric
Owl Appliqués - Assorted scraps		
Four-Patch Block		
Background Assorted scraps each of 4 Fabrics	1*	5¼" square *cut for each fabric
Flower Appliqués - Assorted scraps		
Lady Bug Block		
Fabric A Background ⅙ yard	3	4½" squares
Fabric B Background ⅙ yard	3	4½" squares
Fabric C Background Scrap	2	4½" squares
Lady Bug Appliqués - Assorted scraps		

Large Flower Block		
Fabric A Background ⅛ yard each of 2 Fabrics	4* 8* 8*	2½" squares 1½" squares 1" squares *cut for each fabric
Fabric B Large Petals ⅙ yard each of 2 Fabrics	8* 4* 16*	3" x 2½" 1½" squares 1" squares *cut for each fabric
Fabric C Small Petals ⅙ yard each of 2 Fabrics	1* 8*	3½" square 1½" x 2" *cut for each fabric
Flower Appliqués - Assorted scraps		
Tulip Block		
Fabric A Background ⅙ yard each of 2 Fabrics	2* 2* 4* 2* 2* 1* 2*	2¾" x 3¾" 2½" x 4¾" (PP #6 & 7) 2½" squares 2¼" x 3½" (PP #2 & 3) 1½" x 4¼" (PP #8 & 9) 1¼" x 7½" 1¼" x 3¾" *cut for each fabric (adjust cuts for directional fabric)
Fabric B Tulip Petals Scrap each of 2 Fabrics	1* 1*	3¾" x 3½" (PP #4) 3¾" x 5¾" (PP #5) *cut for each fabric
Fabric C Tulip Center & Stem Scrap each of 2 Fabrics	1* 1*	2" square (PP #1) 1" x 5½" *cut for each fabric
Fabric D Leaves Scrap each of 2 Fabrics	2*	3¾" x 2½" *cut for each fabric
Accent Borders		
Fabric A ⅙ yard	3*	1" x 42"
Fabric B ⅙ yard each of 3 Fabrics	4*	1" x 42" *cut for each fabric
Binding ½ yard	4 1	2¾" x 42" 1" x 42"
Backing - 1 yard Batting - 37" x 36" ⅛" Buttons - 6 for eyes Lightweight Fusible Web - ½ yard Note: Directional fabric not recommended for beginners.		

Fabric Requirements and Cutting
Instructions Read all instructions before beginning and use ¼"-wide seam allowances throughout. Read Cutting Strips and Pieces on page 124 prior to cutting fabric.

Getting Started This garden inspired quilt consists of smaller scaled blocks found in various projects in this book. Refer to Accurate Seam Allowance on page 124. Whenever possible use Assembly Line Method on page 124. Press seams in direction of arrows. Refer to appliqué instructions on page 125. Our instructions are for Quick-Fuse Appliqué, but if you prefer hand appliqué, reverse patterns and add ¼"-wide seam allowances. Appliqués are added to each block prior to sewing the quilt top together.

Making the Owl Blocks

1. Refer to Quick Corner Triangles on page 124. Making quick corner triangle units, sew two 1¼" Fabric B squares to one 2" x 5½" Fabric A piece as shown. Press.

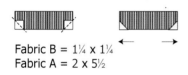

Fabric B = 1¼ x 1¼
Fabric A = 2 x 5½

2. Making quick corner triangles units, sew two 1½" Fabric A squares to one 5½" x 4½" Fabric C piece as shown. Press.

Fabric A = 1½ x 1½
Fabric C = 5½ x 4½

3. Sew together unit from step 1, one 3" x 5½" Fabric B piece, unit from step 2, and one 2" x 5½" Fabric A piece as shown. Press. Sew this unit between two 10" x 1¾" Fabric A strips. Press. Block measures 8" x 10".

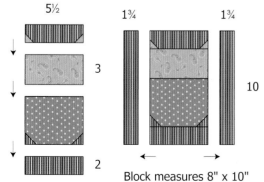

Block measures 8" x 10"

4. Refer to steps 1-3 to make two additional Owl Blocks as shown.

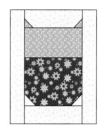 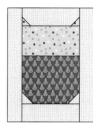

5. Use patterns on page 38 to trace wings, eyes, legs and beaks on paper side of fusible web (quantity needed noted on patterns). Use appropriate fabrics to prepare all appliqués for fusing.

6. Refer to photo on page 32 and layout on page 36 to position and fuse appliqués to quilt. Finish appliqué edges with machine satin stitch or other decorative stitching as desired.

Making the Four-Patch Flower Block

1. Sew two Fabric A squares together. Press. Make two. Sew these units together as shown. Press.

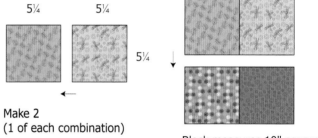

Make 2
(1 of each combination)

Block measures 10" squares

2. Use Owl Appliqué Flower patterns on page 9 to trace four large flowers and four flower centers on paper side of fusible web. Use appropriate fabrics to prepare all appliqués for fusing.

3. Refer to photo on page 33 and layout on page 36 to position and fuse large flower appliqués to block. Finish appliqué edges with machine satin stitch or other decorative stitching as desired.

4. Follow directions on page 8, Layering and Finishing, steps 3-6 to make four dimensional flowers. Center and pin small flower piece to large flowers. Position and fuse flower centers and machine satin stitch or other decorative stitching as desired. Center stitching will hold dimensional petals in place.

Favorite Themes Sampler Quilt
33" x 31½"

Making the Ladybug Block

1. Use pattern on page 38 to trace eight ladybugs on paper side of fusible web. Use appropriate fabrics to prepare all appliqués for fusing.

2. Refer to photo on page 33 and layout to position and fuse appliqués to three 4½" Fabric A squares, three 4½" Fabric B squares, and two 4½" Fabric C squares. Finish appliqué edges with machine satin stitch or other decorative stitching as desired. Note: Keep appliqués away from seam allowance areas.

3. Referring to layout, arrange and sew together eight ladybug units from step 2. Press and label this Row 4.

Making the Large Flower Block

1. Refer to Quick Corner Triangles on page 124. Making quick corner triangle units, sew two 1" Fabric B squares to one 1½" x 2" Fabric C piece as shown. Press. Make eight.

Fabric B = 1 x 1
Fabric C = 1½ x 2
Make 8

2. Sew two units from step 1 together as shown. Press. Make four. Sew one 3½" Fabric C square between two of these units as shown. Press.

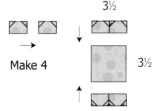

Make 4

3. Sew one small unit from step 2 between two 1½" Fabric B squares as shown. Press. Make two. Sew these units to sides of unit from step 2. Press.

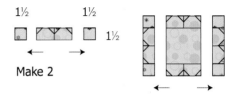

Make 2

4. Making quick corner triangles units, sew one 1" and one 1½" Fabric A square to one 3" x 2½" Fabric B piece as shown. Press. Make eight, four of each variation. Sew two units, one of each variation together as shown. Press. Make four.

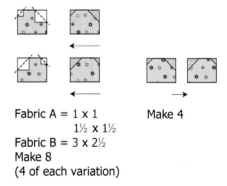

Fabric A = 1 x 1
    1½ x 1½   Make 4
Fabric B = 3 x 2½
Make 8
(4 of each variation)

5. Sew unit from step 3 between two units from step 4 as shown. Press.

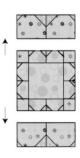

6. Sew one unit from step 4 between two 2½" Fabric A squares as shown. Press. Make two. Sew these units to sides of unit from step 5 as shown. Press. Block measures 9½" square.

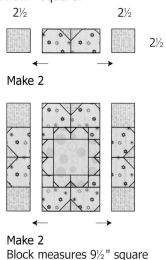

Make 2

Block measures 9½" square

7. Use pattern on page 38 to trace two large flower centers on paper side of fusible web. Use appropriate fabrics to prepare appliqués for fusing. Fuse to center of block. Finish appliqué edges with machine satin stitch or other decorative stitching as desired. Block measures 9½" square. Repeat steps to make one additional Large Flower Block using different fabric combinations.

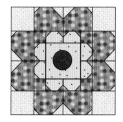

Making the Tulip Block

1. Refer to paper-piecing pattern on page 38 to make two copies following instructions. Refer to Sunny Tulip quilt, Making the Tulip Blocks, (pages 67-68), steps 1-6 for detailed step instructions. To complete paper-pieced section of Tulip Block, add pieces 8 and 9. Trim an outside trim line. Make two using different fabric combinations.

2. Refer to Quick Corner Triangles on page 124. Making quick corner triangle units, sew two 2½" Fabric A squares to one 3¾" x 2½" Fabric D piece as shown. Press. Make two, one of each variation.

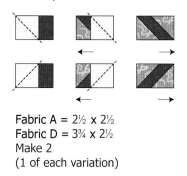

Fabric A = 2½ x 2½
Fabric D = 3¾ x 2½
Make 2
(1 of each variation)

3. Sew one unit from step 2 between one 2¾" x 3¾" and one 1¼" x 3¾" Fabric A pieces as shown. Press. Make two, one of each variation. Sew one 1" x 5½" Fabric C piece between these units as shown.

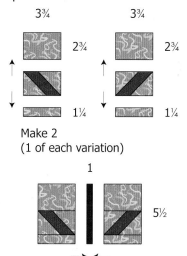

Make 2
(1 of each variation)

4. Arrange and sew together one 1¼" x 7½" Fabric A piece, unit from step 1, and unit from step 3 as shown. Press. Block measures 7½" x 9½". Repeat steps to make one additional Tulip Block using different fabric combinations.

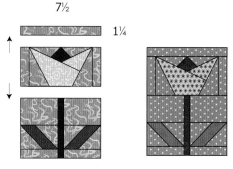

Block measures 7½" x 9½"

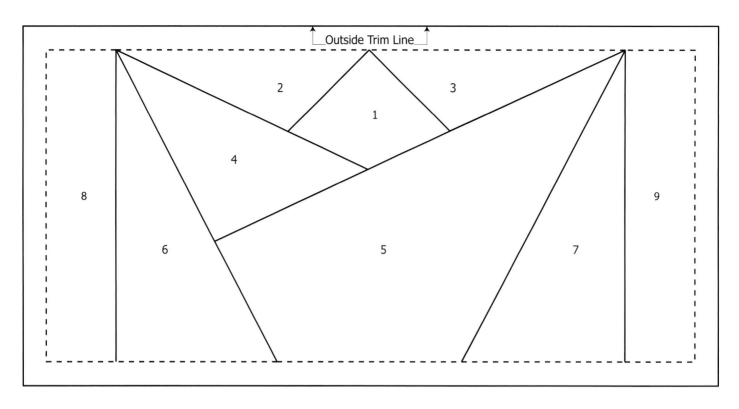

Favorite Themes Sampler Quilt

2 copies are needed for this project. It is recommended to make a few extra copies.
Permission is granted by Debbie Mumm® to copy page 38 to successfully complete the Favorite Themes Sampler Quilt.
Compare copy to the original. Copy should measure 7½" x 3¾". Adjust copier setting if it varies.

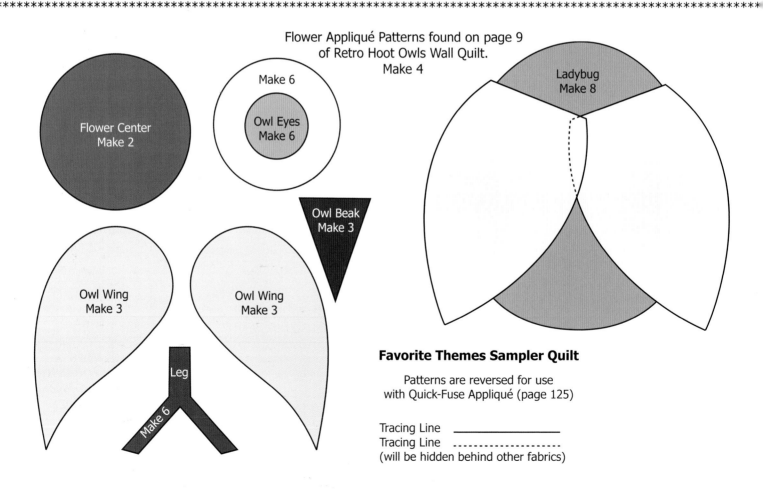

Flower Appliqué Patterns found on page 9
of Retro Hoot Owls Wall Quilt.
Make 4

Make 6

Owl Eyes
Make 6

Ladybug
Make 8

Flower Center
Make 2

Owl Beak
Make 3

Owl Wing
Make 3

Owl Wing
Make 3

Leg

Make 6

Favorite Themes Sampler Quilt

Patterns are reversed for use
with Quick-Fuse Appliqué (page 125)

Tracing Line ——————
Tracing Line - - - - - - - - - - -
(will be hidden behind other fabrics)

Assembling the Quilt

1. Referring to photo on page 33 and layout on page 36, arrange and sew together three Owl Blocks and one Four-Patch Block. Press and label Row 2.

2. Referring to photo on page 33 and layout on page 36, arrange and sew together two Large Flower blocks and two Tulip Blocks. Press and label Row 6.

3. Referring to photo on page 33 and layout on page 36, sew lengthwise various combinations of 1" x 42" Fabric A, B, and binding strips to complete strip sets as shown. Rows 1 and 7 use one Fabric A and one each of Fabric B strips, Row 5 uses one Fabric A strip and one each of Fabric B strips and one 1" binding strip, and Row 3 consists of one Fabric A and two different Fabric B strips. Cut each strips sets into 32½" lengths.

Row 1 & 7
Fabric A & 3 different Fabric B strips

Row 3
Fabric A & 2 different Fabric B strips

Row 5
Fabric A, 3 different Fabric B strips
& one 1" binding strip

4. Referring to photo on page 33 and layout on page 36, arrange and sew rows together. Press.

Layering and Finishing

1. Referring to Layering the Quilt on page 126, arrange and baste backing, batting, and top together. Hand or machine quilt as desired.

2. Refer to Binding the Quilt on page 126. Use 2¾"-wide binding strips to bind quilt.

NOTES FROM Debbie

This modern retro sampler quilt is a compilation of blocks from other quilts in this book that have been gathered together to create something fresh and new. I designed it half scale and that's what makes it so dang cute! In fact, this may be my favorite quilt of the book. The clean look of the "solid–esque" fabrics that create the striped border (along with a playful color story) create this modern, yet retro style.

I've always loved putting a variety of blocks together for sampler quilts. Including this one that was featured in my tenth anniversary book!

1996
Anniversary
Sampler
Originally featured in
10th Anniversary

New Memories

metamorphosis ▪ quilt

New Memories Metamorphosis Quilt Finished Size: 43" x 52½"	FIRST CUT		SECOND CUT	
	Number of Strips or Pieces	Dimensions	Number of Pieces	Dimensions
Fabric A Block Centers ⅙ yard each of 4 Fabrics	1*	3½" x 42" *cut for each fabric	5*	3½" squares
Fabric B Block Small Triangles ⅙ yard each of 4 Fabrics	1*	3" x 42" *cut for each fabric	10*	3" squares** **cut once diagonally
Fabric C Block Medium Triangles ⅙ yard each of 4 Fabrics	1*	4" x 42" *cut for each fabric	10*	4" squares** **cut once diagonally
Fabric D Block 1 Large Triangles ¼ yard each of 4 Fabrics	2*	3½" x 42" *cut for each fabric	4*	3½" x 12"
Fabric D Block 2 Large Triangles ¼ yard each of 4 Fabrics	2*	3½" x 42" *cut for each fabric	4*	3½" x 12"
Fabric D Block 3 Large Triangles ¼ yard each of 4 Fabrics	2*	3½" x 42" *cut for each fabric	4*	3½" x 12"
Fabric D Block 4 Large Triangles ¼ yard each of 4 Fabrics	2*	3½" x 42" *cut for each fabric	4*	3½" x 12"
First Border ¼ yard	5	1" x 42"	2	1" x 38½"
Outside Border ⅓ yard	5	2" x 42"	2	2" x 39½"
Binding ½ yard	5	2¾" x 42"		
Backing - 2¾ yards Batting - 49" x 58"				

Fabric Requirements and Cutting Instructions
Read all instructions before beginning and use ¼"-wide seam allowances throughout. Read Cutting Strips and Pieces on page 124 prior to cutting fabric.

Getting Started
This group of blocks creates a pleasing and stimulating quilt featuring a toss and turn layout. Block measures 10" square (unfinished). Refer to Accurate Seam Allowance on page 124. Whenever possible use Assembly Line Method on page 124. Press seams in direction of arrows.

Making the Blocks
It is recommended to sew one block first to learn the technique. The diagrams show both versions, the right direction (points going clockwise) and the left direction (points going counter-clockwise).

1. Cut four 3½" x 12" Fabric D matching pieces once diagonally as shown. Cut four, two in each direction. Repeat for all remaining 3½" x 12" Fabric D pieces. (Note: There will be a few triangle pieces not used in project.)

Cut 2
Make 4 Right Triangles
Tip points clockwise

Cut 2
Make 4 Left Triangles
Tip points counter-clockwise

2. Sew four Fabric B triangles to one 3½" Fabric A square as shown. Triangle ends will extent past block edges. Press. Square to 4¾".

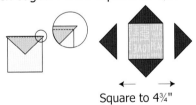

Square to 4¾"

3. Sew four Fabric C triangles to unit from step 2 as shown. Press. Square to 6½".

Square to 6½"

4. Four Block 1 Fabric D triangles will be sewn to unit from step 3. Make sure that all triangle angles are going in the same direction. The first triangle is sewn using a partial seam. Using ¼"-wide seam allowance, start stitching from red dot to outside edge. Mark is approximately 2" from edge. Finger press the sewn area only. The section not sewn will be stitched after all other triangles are sewn.

Right   Left

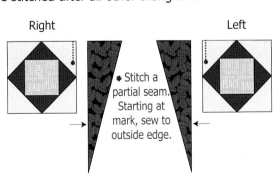

✦ Stitch a partial seam. Starting at mark, sew to outside edge.

5. Place the right angle of a different Fabric D triangle on unit as shown, right sides together. Sew entire length of triangle to unit. Press.

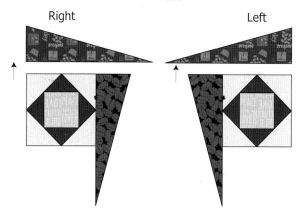

6. Align and stitch a different Fabric D triangle to unit as shown. Press.

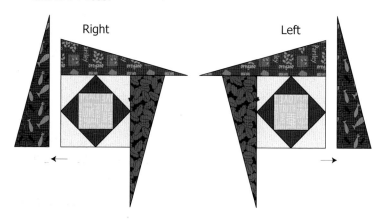

7. Align and stitch the final Fabric D triangle to unit as shown. Press. Finish stitching the first triangle to unit from mark to triangle point. Press.

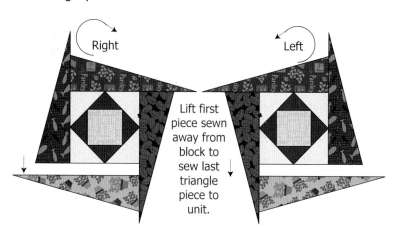

8. Square unit from step 7 to 10", centering block.

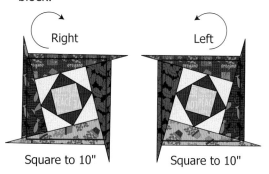

Square to 10"   Square to 10"

9. Repeat steps 2-8 to make five blocks of each fabric combination: Block 1 (three rights and two lefts), Block 2 (two rights and three lefts), Block 3 (two rights and three lefts), and Block 4 (three rights and two lefts).

Block 1   **Block 2**

Make 3 rights & 2 lefts   Make 2 rights & 3 lefts

Block 3   **Block 4**

Make 2 rights & 3 lefts   Make 3 rights & 2 lefts

Assembling the Quilt

The large triangle pieces have bias outside edges. When handling pieces during sewing, be careful not to pull or tug on fabric; instead let the feed dogs guide fabric through the machine.

1. Refer to photo on page 41 and layout on page 43 to arrange blocks into five rows with four blocks each, alternating right and left blocks. Sew blocks together. Press seams in opposite direction from row to row.

2. Sew rows together. Press.

2004 Memories Lap Quilt

Originally featured in Creative Woman

Many, many of our old memories are wonderful. However, sometimes in life we must wipe the slate clean, and make New Memories. Have you ever had a signature quilt that, for whatever reason, no longer applies? So, why not make a new quilt and call it New Memories and even make it using new and different techniques? Our original Memories Quilt was made in 2004 for my Creative Woman book with much love, but I realize now that the technique we used wasted too much fabric. We all learn from life (and sewing), right? So, re-invent yourself and create new memories while you make this slightly twisted quilt that comes with a slightly twisted tale.

New Memories Metamorphosis Quilt

43" x 52½"

Adding the Borders

1. Refer to Adding the Borders on page 126. Sew two 1" x 38½" First Border strips to top and bottom of quilt. Press seams toward border.

2. Sew 1" x 42" First Border strips together end-to-end to make one continuous 1"-wide First Border strip. Press. Measure quilt through center from top to bottom including borders just added. Cut two 1"-wide First Border strips to this measurement. Sew to sides of quilt. Press.

3. Sew two 2" x 39½" Outside Border strips to top and bottom of quilt. Press seams toward border just sewn. Refer to step 2 to join, measure, trim, and sew 2"-wide Outside Border strips sides of quilt. Press.

Layering and Finishing

1. Cut backing crosswise into two equal pieces. Sew pieces together lengthwise to make one 49" x 80" (approximate) backing piece. Press and trim to 49" x 58".

2. Referring to Layering the Quilt on page 126, arrange and baste backing, batting, and top together. Hand or machine quilt as desired.

3. Refer to Binding the Quilt on page 126. Sew 2¾" x 42" binding strips end-to-end to make one continuous 2¾"-wide binding strip. Bind quilt to finish.

In the Jungle
family room ▪ quilt

In the Jungle Family Room Quilt Finished Size: 67" x 81"	FIRST CUT		SECOND CUT	
	Number of Strips or Pieces	Dimensions	Number of Pieces	Dimensions
Fabric A Beginning Square ¼ yard	2	3½" x 42"	20	3½" squares
Fabric B Block 1st Border ⅓ yard	5	1½" x 42"	20 20	1½" x 4½" 1½" x 3½"
Fabric C Block 2nd Border ½ yard	6	2½" x 42"	20 20	2½" x 6½" 2½" x 4½"
Fabric D Block 3rd Border ½ yard	8	1½" x 42"	20 20	1½" x 7½" 1½" x 6½"
Fabric E Block 4th Border ½ yard	9	1½" x 42"	20 20	1½" x 8½" 1½" x 7½"
Fabric F Block 5th Border ½ yard	10	1½" x 42"	20 20	1½" x 9½" 1½" x 8½"
Fabric G Block 6th Border 1 yard	12	2½" x 42"	20 20	2½" x 11½" 2½" x 9½"
Fabric H Block 7th Border ¾ yard	14	1½" x 42"	20 20	1½" x 12½" 1½" x 11½"
Fabric I Block 1 Border ¾ yard	9	2½" x 42"	10 10	2½" x 14½" 2½" x 12½"
Fabric J Block 2 Border ¾ yard	9	2½" x 42"	10 10	2½" x 14½" 2½" x 12½"
First Border ⅜ yard	7	1½" x 42"		
Second Border ⅜ yard	7	1½" x 42"		
Third Border ¼ yard	7	1" x 42"		
Outside Border ⅞ yard	8	3" x 42"		
Binding ¾ yard	8	2¾" x 42"		
Backing - 5 yards Batting - 75" x 89"				

Fabric Requirements and Cutting Instructions
Read all instructions before beginning and use ¼"-wide seam allowances throughout. Read Cutting Strips and Pieces on page 124 prior to cutting fabric.

Getting Started
Go to the wild side by using animal fabric prints to create this adventure quilt. Block measures 14½" square. Refer to Accurate Seam Allowance on page 124. Whenever possible use Assembly Line Method on page 124. Press seams in direction of arrows.

Making the Blocks

1. Sew one 3½" Fabric A square to one 1½" x 3½" Fabric B piece as shown. Press. Sew this unit to one 1½" x 4½" Fabric B piece. Press. Make twenty.

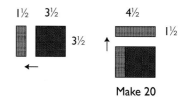

Make 20

2. Sew one 2½" x 4½" Fabric C piece to one unit from step 1 as shown. Press. Sew this unit to one 2½" x 6 ½" Fabric C piece. Press. Make twenty.

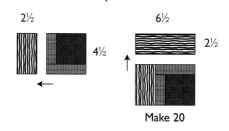

Make 20

In the Jungle Family Room Quilt
67" x 81"

5. Sew one 1½" x 8½" Fabric F piece to one unit from step 4 as shown. Press. Sew this unit to one 1½" x 9½" Fabric F piece. Press. Make twenty.

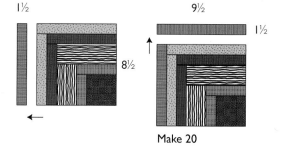

Make 20

6. Sew one 2½" x 9½" Fabric G strip to one unit from step 5 as shown. Press. Sew this unit to one 2½" x 11½" Fabric G strip. Press. Make twenty.

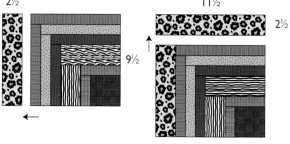

Make 20

7. Sew one 1½" x 11½" Fabric H strip to one unit from step 6 as shown. Press. Sew this unit to one 1½" x 12½" Fabric H strip. Press. Make twenty.

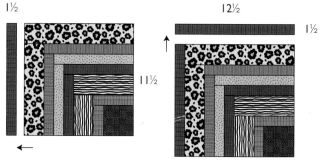

Make 20

3. Sew one 1½" x 6½" Fabric D piece to one unit from step 2 as shown. Press. Sew this unit to one 1½" x 7½" Fabric D piece. Press. Make twenty.

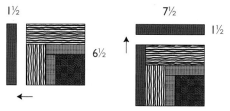

Make 20

4. Sew one 1½" x 7½" Fabric E piece to one unit from step 3 as shown. Press. Sew this unit to one 1½" x 8½" Fabric E piece. Press. Make twenty.

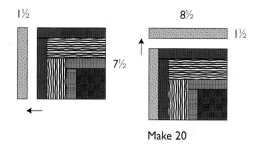

Make 20

8. Sew one 2½" x 12½" Fabric I strip to one unit from step 7 as shown. Press. Sew this unit to one 2½" x 14½" Fabric I strip. Press. Make ten. Label Block 1. Block measures 14½" square.

Block 1

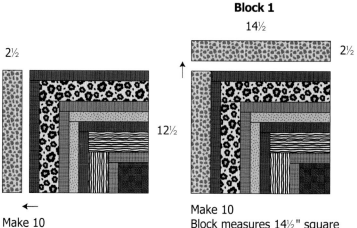

Make 10

Make 10
Block measures 14½" square

9. Sew one 2½" x 12½" Fabric J strip to one unit from step 7 as shown. Press. Sew this unit to one 2½" x 14½" Fabric J strip. Press. Make ten. Label Block 2. Block measures 14½" square.

Block 2

14½

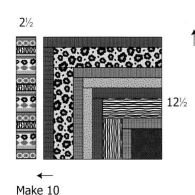

2½

12½

2½

←
Make 10

Make 10
Block measures 14½" square

10. Referring to photo on page 45 and layout on page 46, arrange and sew together five rows with four blocks each, two of each variation alternating Block 1 and 2 placement from row to row. Press seams opposite from row to row. Sew rows together. Press.

Adding the Borders

1. Sew 1½" x 42" First Border strips together end-to-end to make one continuous 1½"-wide First Border strip. Referring to Adding the Borders on page 126, measure quilt through center from side to side. Cut two 1½"-wide First Border strips to this measurement. Sew to top and bottom of quilt. Press seams toward border.

2. Measure quilt through center from top to bottom including border just added. Cut two 1½"-wide First Border strips to this measurement. Sew to sides of quilt. Press.

3. Refer to steps 1 and 2 to join, measure, trim and sew 1½"-wide Second Border, 1"- wide Third Border, and 3"-wide Outside Border strips to top, bottom and sides of quilt. Press.

Layering and Finishing

1. Cut backing crosswise into two equal pieces. Sew pieces together lengthwise to make one 90" x 80" (approximate) backing piece.

2. Referring to Layering the Quilt on page 126, arrange and baste backing, batting and top together. Hand or machine quilt as desired.

3. Refer to Binding the Quilt on page 126. Sew 2¾" x 42" binding strips end-to-end to make one continuous 2¾"-wide binding strip. Bind quilt to finish.

NOTES FROM Debbie

This quilt migrated from the sea shore to the jungle ~ quite a transformation! In fact, you'd probably never guess these two quilts were made from the same pattern. Sea to Shore featured soothing blues and tans when I designed it for Colors from Nature in 2008. Today, animal patterns like zebra stripes and cheetah spots are very popular so I created a fabric line in the jungle theme and tried to use as many of the prints as I could in this fun quilt. I think that this quilt will appeal to the fellas in the family! This design will make everyone in the family squabble over whose lap it covers while cozying up on the sofa to watch a favorite TV program.

2008
Sea to Shore
Originally featured in
Colors from
Nature

Wheels of Creativity

lap ■ quilt

Wheels of Creativity Lap Quilt Finished Size: 46" x 59"	FIRST CUT		SECOND CUT	
	Number of Strips or Pieces	Dimensions	Number of Pieces	Dimensions
Fabric A Block Triangles ⅞ yard each of 2 Fabrics	8*	3½" x 42" *cut for each fabric	48*	3½" x 6½"
Fabric B Block Small Triangles ⅝ yard each of 3 Fabrics	5*	3½" x 42" *cut for each fabric	48*	3½" squares
Fabric C Color Triangle Accents ¼ yard each of 4 Fabrics	2*	3½" x 42" *cut for each fabric	12*	3½" squares
Fabric D Cornerstones ⅛ yard	1	1½" x 42"	20	1½" squares
Fabric E Sashing ⅝ yard	11	1½" x 42"	31	1½" x 12½"
First Border ¼ yard	5	1" x 42"		
Outside Border ½ yard	5	2½" x 42"		
Binding ⅝ yard	6	2¾" x 42"		
Backing - 3 yards Batting - 52" x 65"				

Fabric Requirements and Cutting Instructions

Read all instructions before beginning and use ¼"-wide seam allowances throughout. Read Cutting Strips and Pieces on page 124 prior to cutting fabric.

Getting Started

Sparks of color add fun to this striking black and white quilt. Block measures 12½" square (unfinished). Refer to Accurate Seam Allowance on page 124. Whenever possible use Assembly Line Method on page 124. Press seams in direction of arrows.

Making the Block

1. Refer to Quick Corner Triangles on page 124 . Making quick corner triangle units, sew two different 3½" Fabric B squares to one 3½" x 6½" Fabric A piece as shown. Press. Make twelve matching units.

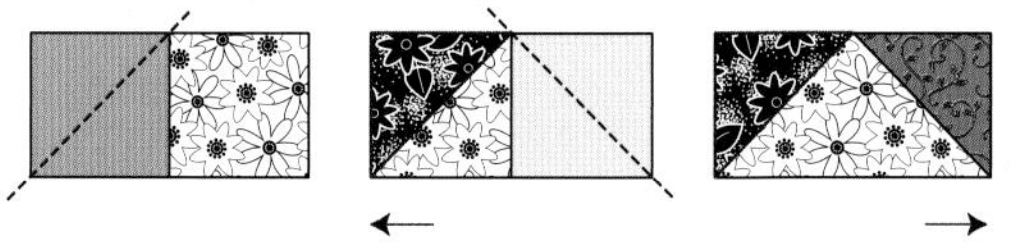

Fabric B = 3½ x 3½
Fabric A = 3½ x 6½
Make 12

2. Making quick corner triangle units, sew one 3½" Fabric B square and one 3½" Fabric C square to one 3½" x 6½" Fabric A piece as shown. Press. Make twelve matching units.

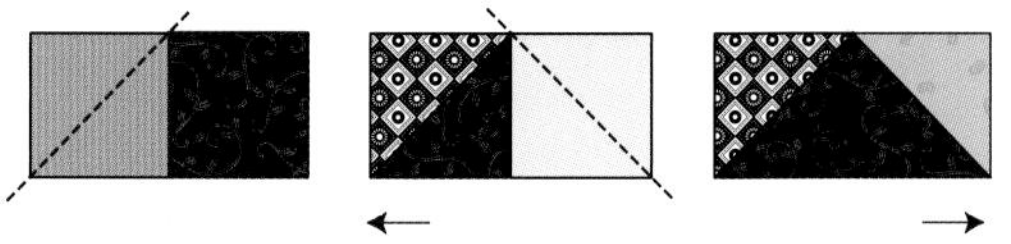

Fabric B = 3½ x 3½
Fabric C = 3½ x 3½
Fabric A = 3½ x 6½
Make 12

Wheels of Creativity Lap Quilt
46" x 59"

5. Sew two units from step 4 together in pairs as shown. Refer to Twisting seams on page 124 and press. Make three. Block measures 12½" square.

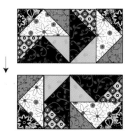

Make 3
Block measures 12½" square

6. Repeat steps 1-5 to make nine additional blocks for a total of twelve blocks, three of each Fabric C combination.

Make 3   Make 3

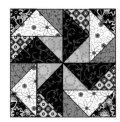

Make 3

Assembling the Quilt

1. Refer to photo on page 49 and layout to arrange all blocks and sashing pieces into rows prior to sewing.

3. Sew one unit from step 1 to one unit from step 2 as shown. Press. Make twelve.

Make 12

4. Sew two units from step 3 together as shown. Press. Make six.

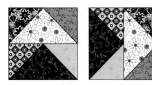

Make 6

2. Sew four 1½" Fabric D squares and three 1½" x 12½" Fabric E strips together as shown. Press. Make five rows.

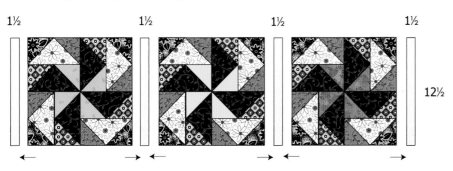

Make 5

3. Sew four 1½" x 12½" Fabric E strips and three assorted blocks together as shown. Press. Make four rows.

Make 4

4. Referring to photo on page 49 and layout on page 50, arrange and sew together rows from step 2 and 3. Press.

Adding the Borders

1. Refer to Adding the Borders on page 126. Measure quilt through center from side to side. Cut two 1"-wide First Border strips to this measurement. Sew to top and bottom of quilt. Press seams toward border.

2. Sew 1" x 42" First Border strips together end-to-end to make one continuous 1"-wide First Border strip. Measure quilt through center from top to bottom including borders just added. Cut two 1"-wide First Border strips to this measurement. Sew to sides of quilt. Press.

3. Refer to steps 1 and 2 to join, measure, trim, and sew 2½"-wide Outside Border strips to top, bottom, and sides of quilt. Press.

Layering and Finishing

1. Cut backing crosswise into two equal pieces. Sew pieces together lengthwise to make one 52" x 80" (approximate) backing piece. Press and trim to 52" x 65".

2. Referring to Layering the Quilt on page 126, arrange and baste backing, batting, and top together. Hand or machine quilt as desired.

3. Refer to Binding the Quilt on page 126. Sew 2¾" x 42" binding strips end-to-end to make one continuous 2¾"-wide binding strip. Bind quilt to finish.

I gave this quilt a whole new spin! The original quilt featured a restful combination of lavenders and greens and was titled "Remembrance." It was created with empathy for families affected by Alzheimer's for our book, I Care with Quilts (2009). The importance of this quilt was punctuated by the fact that Kris Clifford, my long-time assistant, was dealing with this disease in her own family. Lavender is the signature color for Alzheimer's and the color combination and organization of this quilt seem to inspire peace of mind. My new version, however, is very different in the emotional response it evokes - it's almost frenetically active! Every block is in motion and doing it's own thing...like when you've had too much caffeine! When I look at this quilt I imagine a creative, yet organized mind in action. You know, like a quilter!

2009
Remembrance
Originally featured in I Care with Quilts

Random Red & White
throw ■ quilt

Random Red & White Throw Quilt Finished Size: 43" x 55"	FIRST CUT	
	Number of Strips or Pieces	Dimensions
Block 1 Fat Quarter each of 4 Fabrics A B C D	4*	8" squares *cut for each fabric
Block 2 Fat Quarter each of 4 Fabrics A B C D	4*	8" squares *cut for each fabric
Block 3 Fat Quarter each of 4 Fabrics A B C D	4*	8" squares *cut for each fabric
Block 4 Fat Quarter each of 4 Fabrics A B C D	4*	8" squares *cut for each fabric
Binding ⅝ yard	6	2¾" x 42"
Backing - 2¾ yards Batting - 49" x 61"		

Fabric Requirements and Cutting Instructions
Read all instructions before beginning and use ¼"-wide seam allowances throughout. Read Cutting Strips and Pieces on page 124 prior to cutting fabric.

Getting Started
Sixteen coordinating white and shades of red quarter-square triangles gives this quilt a great scrappy and cheery look. Block measures 6½" square. Refer to Accurate Seam Allowance on page 124. Whenever possible use Assembly Line Method on page 124. Press seams in direction of arrows.

Making the Blocks

1. Draw a diagonal line on wrong side of one 8" Block 1, Fabric A square. Place marked square and one 8" Block 1 Fabric B square right sides together. Sew scant ¼" away from drawn line on both sides to make half-square triangles as shown. Make four matching units. Cut on drawn line and press seams open. This will make eight half-square A/B triangle units for Block 1.

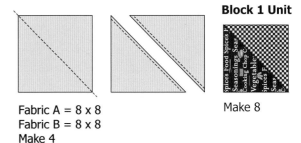

Fabric A = 8 x 8
Fabric B = 8 x 8
Make 4

Block 1 Unit
Make 8

2. Repeat step 1 to make eight half-square triangles for each A/B fabric combination for Block 2, Block 3, and Block 4 units.

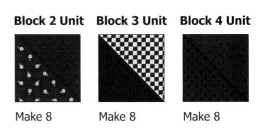

Block 2 Unit   **Block 3 Unit**   **Block 4 Unit**
Make 8   Make 8   Make 8

Random Red & White Throw Quilt
43" x 55"

4. Repeat step 3 to make eight half-square triangles for each C/D fabric combination for Block 2, Block 3, and Block 4 units.

Block 2 Unit	Block 3 Unit	Block 4 Unit
Make 8	Make 8	Make 8

5. Draw a diagonal line on wrong side of one Block 1 unit from step 1 in opposite direction from seam as shown. Place marked unit right sides together with one Block 1 unit from step 3 placing Fabric A triangle on top of Fabric C triangle and Fabric B triangle on top of Fabric D triangle. Sew scant ¼" away form drawn line on both sides. Make eight using Block 1 units. Cut on drawn line and press seams open. Square to 6½". This will make sixteen quarter-square triangles, eight of each variation. Sort and label Block 1 and Block 1R (reversed) as shown. Note: To get additional variety in fabric placement within Block 1, place some Fabric A triangles on top of Fabric D triangles.

		Block 1	Block 1R

Unit from step 1
Unit from step 3
Make 8

Make 16
(8 of each variation)
Square to 6½"

3. Draw a diagonal line on wrong side of one 8" Block 1 Fabric C square. Place marked square and one 8" Block 1 Fabric D square right sides together. Sew scant ¼" away from drawn line on both sides to make half-square triangles as shown. Make four matching units. Cut on drawn line and press seams open. This will make eight half-square C/D triangle units for Block 1. Note: We marked a diagonal line on the lighter square and matched it with an unmarked fabric square.

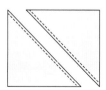

Block 1 Unit

Fabric D = 8 x 8
Fabric C = 8 x 8
Make 4

Make 8

6. Repeat step 5 to make quarter-square triangles using units from steps 2 and 4 for Block 2, Block 3, and Block 4. Sort and label each combination Block 2, 2R, 3, 3R, 4, or 4R as shown.

Block 2	Block 2R	Block 3	Block 3R

Make 16
(8 of each variation)
Square to 6½"

Make 16
(8 of each variation)
Square to 6½"

Block 4	Block 4R

Make 16
(8 of each variation)
Square to 6½"

2005
Bountiful Harvest
Originally featured in
Seasons

Triangles and more triangles ~ and they aren't even arranged in any particular order. It is such a simple concept, and yet such a classic. I think that is why this quilt, originally named Bountiful Harvest from our 2005 Seasons book has always been a staff favorite. It's that classic simplicity that particularly appealed to Carolyn Ogden who has been my Managing Editor for many Debbie Mumm titles. Carolyn and I often joke that we are becoming the same person since we have such similar taste. More than a few times we have purchased the same decorator items without realizing it. She calls me when she's out shopping and sees something that she just knows I will like. Red has always been Carolyn's favorite color and I know she'll love it paired up with her favorite quilt.

Assembling the Quilt
Since this quilt has a scrappy look, layout all blocks into rows prior to sewing quilt top. Refer to photo on page 53 and layout on page 54.

1. Arrange and sew nine rows with seven blocks each. Press seams in opposite directions from row to row.

Make 9
(in assorted combinations)

2. Sew rows together. Press.

Layering and Finishing

1. Cut backing crosswise into two equal pieces. Sew pieces together lengthwise to make one 49" x 80" (approximate) backing piece. Press and trim to 49" x 61".

2. Referring to Layering the Quilt on page 126, arrange and baste backing, batting, and top together. Hand or machine quilt as desired.

3. Refer to Binding the Quilt on page 126. Sew 2¾" x 42" binding strips end-to-end to make one continuous 2¾"-wide binding strip. Bind quilt to finish.

Crazy Daisies

throw ■ quilt

Crazy Daisies Throw Quilt Finished Size: 55½" x 55½"	FIRST CUT		SECOND CUT	
	Number of Strips or Pieces	Dimensions	Number of Pieces	Dimensions
Fabric A Flower Background Dark ⅔ yard	2	11" x 42"	6	11" squares
Fabric B Flower Background Light ⅔ yard	2	11" x 42"	6	11" squares
Fabric C Maze Block 2 yards*	1 6	13" x 42" 58" x 6½" Cut 13" x 42" strip first from fabric then other strips.		
First Border ¼ yard	5	1¼" x 42"		
Second Border ⅓ yard	6	1¼" x 42"		
Outside Border ½ yard	6	2½" x 42"		
Binding ⅝ yard	6	2¾" x 42"		

Flower Petals - ⅞ yard
Flower Centers - ⅛ yard
Backing - 3½ yards
Batting - 63" x 63"
Lightweight Fusible Web - 2 yards
Template Plastic, Pattern Paper or Heavy Card Stock
*For directional fabric, the size that is listed first runs parallel to selvage.

Fabric Requirements and Cutting Instructions
Read all instructions before beginning and use ¼"-wide seam allowances throughout. Read Cutting Strips and Pieces on page 124 prior to cutting fabric.

Getting Started
These complicated-looking Maze blocks are easy to make by "Fussy Cutting" stripe fabric and sewing a few simple seams. Daisy Blocks add a fun element to this simple quilt. Blocks measure 10" square (unfinished). Refer to Accurate Seam Allowance on page 124. Whenever possible use Assembly Line Method on page 124. Press seams in direction of arrows.

Making the Daisy Block
Refer to appliqué instructions on page 125. Our instructions are for Quick-Fuse Appliqué, but if you prefer hand appliqué, reverse patterns and add ¼"-wide seam allowances.

1. Draw a diagonal line on wrong side of one 11" Fabric B square. Place marked square and one 11" Fabric A square right sides together. Sew scant ¼" away from drawn line on both sides to make half-square triangles as shown. Make six. Cut on drawn line and press. This will make twelve half-square triangle units.

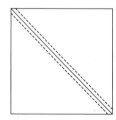

Fabric A = 11 x 11
Fabric B = 11 x 11
Make 6

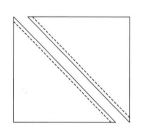

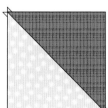

Make 12
Half-square Triangles
Units

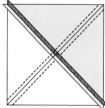

Just one colorful striped fabric can take a dazed daisy (circa 2005 Seasons) and make it crazy! I love the action of stripes when you slice, dice, and reconfigure them. My multi-color, fruit-striped fabric might not be considered the most likely candidate for this quilt, but by using it, I was able to create a lot of vibrancy and movement. When I'm choosing fabrics for a quilt, I love to experiment with out-of-the-box choices, to see if I can achieve an unexpected look. (I also kind of enjoy a raised eyebrow reaction!) In fact, I experiment a lot by viewing an assortment of different choices. Nancy, my fantastic seamstress, calls it "holding auditions." My flannel wall is the stage where various fabrics "try out" before I cast the final choices that will star in the quilt.

2005
Daisy Daze
Originally featured in Seasons

2. Draw a diagonal line on wrong side of one unit from step 1 in opposite direction from seam as shown. Place marked unit and one unmarked unit from step 1, right sides together, matching seams and placing Fabric A triangle on top of Fabric B triangle. Sew a scant ¼" away from drawn line on both sides. Make six. Cut on drawn line and press seam open. Square units to 10". This will make twelve quarter-square triangle units.

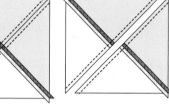

Unit from step 1
Make 6

Square to 10"
Make 12
Quarter-square Triangles Units

3. Use patterns on page 64 to trace ninety-six daisy petals and twelve flower centers on paper side of fusible web. Use appropriate fabrics to prepare all appliqués for fusing.

4. Position and fuse appliqués to twelve units from step 2. Finish appliqué edges with machine satin stitch or other decorative stitching as desired.

Make 12

Making the Maze Block

1. Referring to triangle pattern on page 64, draw pattern on template plastic, pattern paper or heavy card stock. Cut out template and trace four triangles on 58" x 6½" Fabric C strip, aligning top edge with stripe, and centering the same fabric motif at triangle point as shown. This will make one Maze block. Invert pattern and draw another set of triangles, aligning bottom edge with stripe and centering the fabric motif. Repeat to make a total of fifty-two triangles or thirteen sets of four matching triangles. Note: Twelve blocks can be cut from six 58" x 6½" strips. Use 13" x 42" strip to cut four matching striped pieces for the last block.

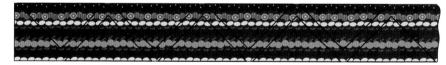

2. Sew matching triangles from step 1 together in pairs. Press seams open. Make twenty-six. Sew two matching pairs of triangle units together to make the Maze Block. Make thirteen. Square blocks to 10" square.

Make 26

Square to 10"
Make 13
Quarter-square Triangles Units

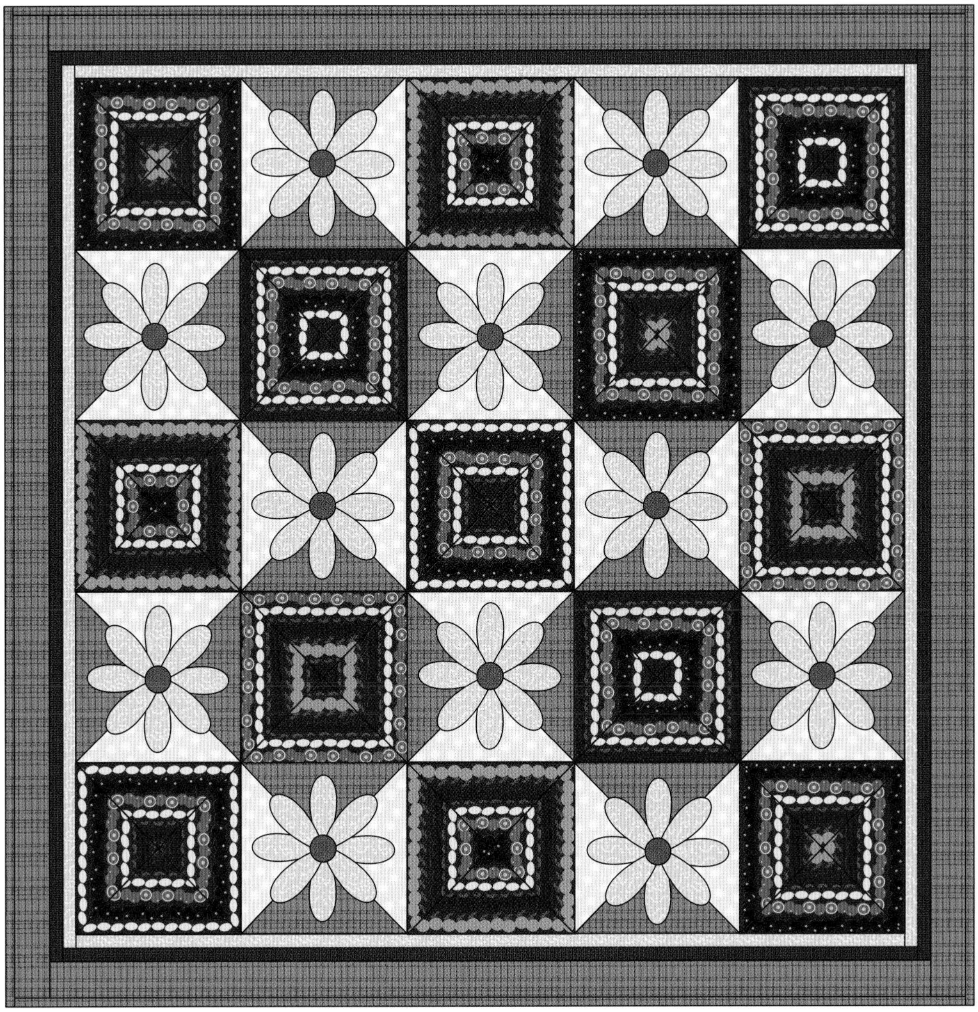

Crazy Daisies Throw Quilt
55½" x 55½"

Assembling the Quilt

1. Arrange and sew together three Maze Blocks and two Daisy Blocks as shown. Press toward Maze blocks. Make three.

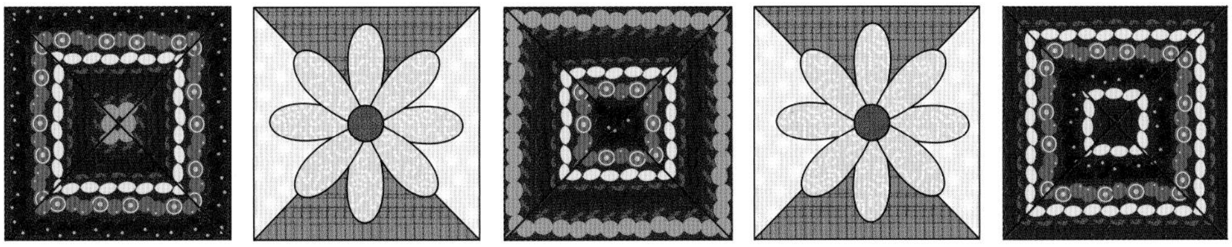

Make 3

2. Arrange and sew together three Daisy Blocks and two Maze Blocks as shown. Press toward Maze blocks. Make two.

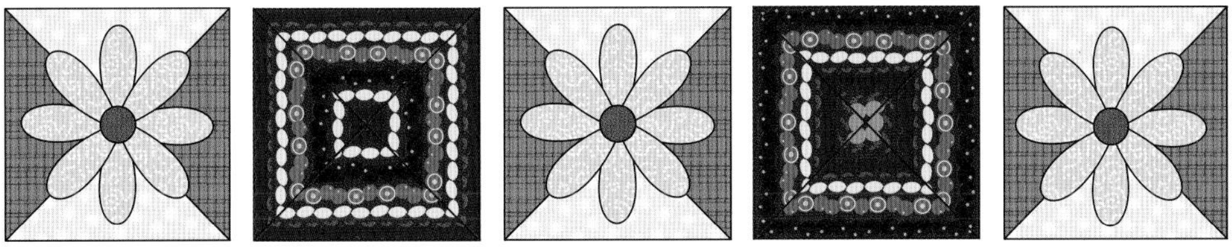

Make 2

3. Referring to photo on page 57 and layout, arrange and sew together rows from steps 1 and 2. Press.

Adding the Borders

1. Refer to Adding the Borders on page 126. Sew 1¼" x 42" First Border strips together end-to-end to make one continuous 1¼"-wide First Border strip. Measure quilt through center from side to side. Cut two 1¼"-wide First Border strips to this measurement. Sew to top and bottom of quilt. Press seams toward border.

2. Measure quilt through center from top to bottom including borders just added. Cut two 1¼"-wide First Border strips to this measurement. Sew to sides of quilt. Press.

3. Refer to steps 1 and 2 to join, measure, trim, and sew 1¼"-wide Second Border strips, and 2½"-wide Outside Border strips to top, bottom, and sides of quilt. Press.

Layering and Finishing

1. Cut backing crosswise into two equal pieces. Sew pieces together lengthwise to make one 63" x 80" (approximate) backing piece. Press and trim to 63" x 63".

2. Referring to Layering the Quilt on page 126, arrange and baste backing, batting, and top together. Hand or machine quilt as desired.

3. Refer to Binding the Quilt on page 126. Sew 2¾" x 42" binding strips end-to-end to make one continuous 2¾"-wide binding strip. Bind quilt to finish.

Friendly Daisies

throw ■ quilt

Friendly Daisies Throw Quilt Finished Size: 35" x 44"	FIRST CUT		SECOND CUT	
	Number of Strips or Pieces	Dimensions	Number of Pieces	Dimensions
Fabric A Flower Background Dark ⅔ yard	2	11" x 42"	6	11" squares
Fabric B Flower Background Light ⅔ yard	2	11" x 42"	6	11" squares
First Border ⅙ yard	4	1" x 42"	2 2	1" x 37½" 1" x 27½"
Outside Border ¼ yard each of 8 Fabrics	3*	1½" x 42" *cut for each fabric	1*	1½" x 21"
Binding ⅜ yard	4	2¾" x 42"		
Flower Petals - ⅞ yard Flower Centers - ⅛ yard Backing - 1½ yards Batting - 41" x 50" Lightweight Fusible Web - 2 yards				

Fabric Requirements and Cutting Instructions Read all instructions before beginning and use ¼"-wide seam allowances throughout. Read Cutting Strips and Pieces on page 124 prior to cutting fabric.

Getting Started Love the Crazy Daisy Quilt on page 56? Here's a smaller version to decorate your wall. Block measures 9½" square (unfinished). Refer to Accurate Seam Allowance on page 124. Whenever possible use Assembly Line Method on page 124. Press seams in direction of arrows.

Making the Daisy Block Refer to appliqué instructions on page 125. Our instructions are for Quick-Fuse Appliqué, but if you prefer hand appliqué, reverse patterns and add ¼"-wide seam allowances.

1. Draw a diagonal line on wrong side of one 11" Fabric B square. Place marked square and one 11" Fabric A square right sides together. Sew scant ¼" away from drawn line on both sides to make half-square triangles as shown. Make six. Cut on drawn line and press. This will make twelve half-square triangle units, six of each variation.

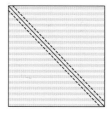
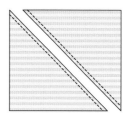
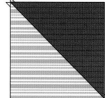
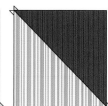

Fabric A = 11 x 11
Fabric B = 11 x 11
Make 6

Make 12
(6 of each variation)
Half-square Triangles Units

Friendly Daisies Throw Quilt
35" x 44"

3. Use patterns on page 64 to trace ninety-six daisy petals and twelve flower centers on paper side of fusible web. Use appropriate fabrics to prepare all appliqués for fusing.

4. Position and fuse appliqués to twelve units from step 2. Finish appliqué edges with machine satin stitch or other decorative stitching as desired.

Make 6   Make 6

Assembling and Adding the Borders

1. Arrange and sew three Daisy Blocks together as shown, checking Fabric B stripe direction prior to sewing. Press seams in opposite directions from row to row. Make four, two of each variation.

2. Referring to photo on page 61 and layout, arrange and sew rows from step 1 together. Press.

3. Sew two 1" x 27½" First Border strips to top and bottom of quilt. Press seams toward border. Sew two 1" x 37½" First Border strips to sides. Press.

4. Sew lengthwise eight 1½" x 42" Outside Border strips, one of each fabric, to make a strip set. Press seams in one direction. Make two. Cut strip set into fifty-two 1½"-wide segments as shown. Repeat step to sew eight 1½" x 21" Outside Border strips together. Press. Cut strip set into thirteen 1½"-wide segments.

2. Draw a diagonal line on wrong side of one unit from step 1 in opposite direction from seam as shown. Place marked unit and one unmarked unit from step 1, right sides together, matching seams and placing Fabric A triangle on top of Fabric B triangle. Sew a scant ¼" away from drawn line on both sides. Make six. Cut on drawn line and press seam open. Square to 9½". This will make twelve quarter-square triangle units, six of each variation.

1½

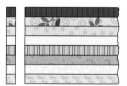

Make 2 using 42" strips
Cut 52 segments

Make 1 using 21" strips
Cut 13 segments

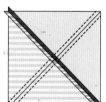 

Unit from step 1
Make 6

Square to 9½"
Make 12
(6 of each variation)
Quarter-square Triangles Units

**2005
Daisy Daze**
Originally featured in
Seasons

Meg Ryan's character in "You've Got Mail" said that daisies were her favorite flower because they are so friendly, and I have to agree. That is why I ended up doing two quilts featuring the daisy for this book. Actually, I couldn't decide which version I liked better and since they were so different, I included both. It's good to be reminded that there are many ways to interpret a design. I chose to use the wrong side of several of the ivory fabrics to keep the contrast and busy-ness down on the border. I also used the back side of the fabric for the daisy petals. When you applique a light fabric over a darker fabric the lighter fabric becomes somewhat transparent and you can often see the darker fabric through it. This is hard to avoid. To counter-balance this, I asked our quilter, Anita, to really emphasize the daisy in this design. She incorporated the cute little swirly-que in the daisy and did echo quilting around the daisy shape. She did a fantastic job and achieved my goal of making these shy daisies really shine.

---

5. Arrange and sew together four segments from step 3 as shown. Press. Make six, press three as shown and three in opposite direction.

Make 6
(Press 3 as shown and 3 in opposite direction.)

6. Referring to photo on page 61 and layout on page 62, arrange three horizontal rows from step 4. Note: Strips are longer than needed to allow for placement options. Stagger rows so the same fabric doesn't touch each other. Measure quilt from side to side. Use this measurement for strip length. Determine the beginning and ending of each row and remove extra pieces. Sew rows together. Press. Make two. Sew to top and bottom of quilt. Press.

7. Arrange and sew together six segments from step 3 as shown. Press. Make six, press three as shown and three in opposite direction.

Make 6
(Press 3 as shown and 3 in opposite direction.)

8. Referring to photo on page 61 and layout on page 62, arrange three vertical rows from step 6. Note: Strips are longer than needed to allow for placement options. Stagger rows so the same fabric doesn't touch each other. Measure quilt from side to side. Use this measurement for strip length. Determine the beginning and ending of each row and remove extra pieces. Sew rows together. Press. Make two. Sew to sides of quilt. Press.

9. Stay-stitch outer edge of quilt top to keep quilt top stable for quilting.

Layering and Finishing

1. Referring to Layering the Quilt on page 126, arrange and baste backing, batting, and top together. Hand or machine quilt as desired.

2. Refer to Binding the Quilt on page 126. Sew 2¾" x 42" binding strips end-to-end to make one continuous 2¾"-wide binding strip. Bind quilt to finish.

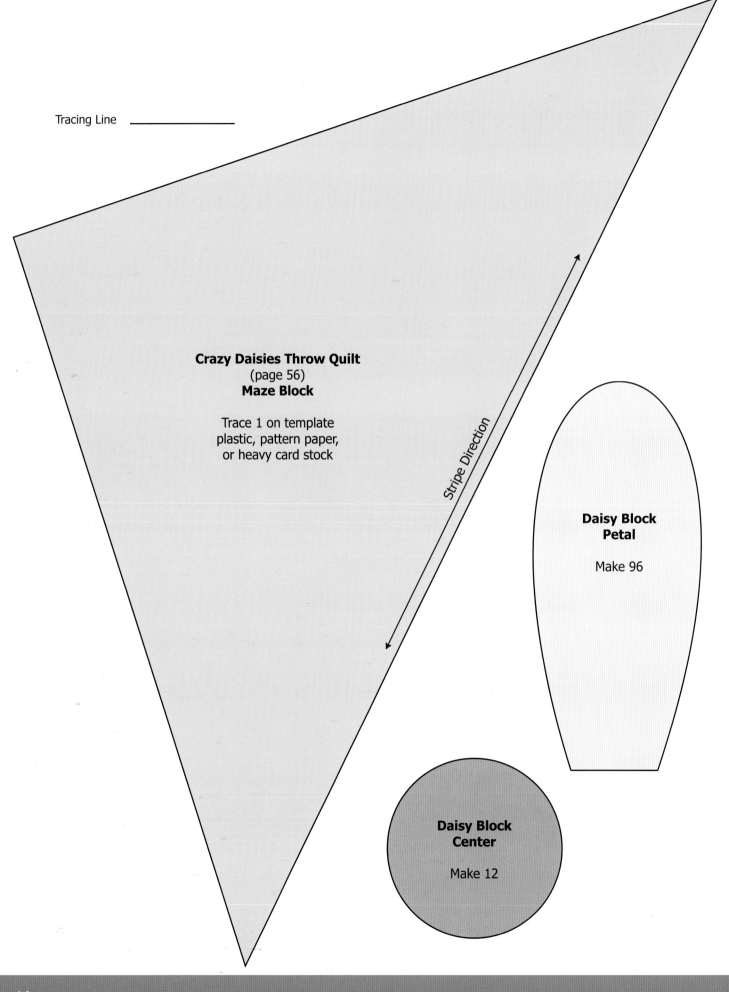

Tracing Line

Crazy Daisies Throw Quilt
(page 56)
Maze Block

Trace 1 on template
plastic, pattern paper,
or heavy card stock

Stripe Direction

**Daisy Block
Petal**

Make 96

**Daisy Block
Center**

Make 12

Sunny Tulips

bed ▪ quilt

Sunny Tulips Bed Quilt Finished Size: 87½" x 97½"	FIRST CUT		SECOND CUT	
	Number of Strips or Pieces	Dimensions	Number of Pieces	Dimensions
Fabric A Four-Patch ⅛ yard each of 9 Fabrics	1*	3" x 42" *cut for each fabric		
Fabric B Background 4½ yards	12	4½" x 42"	56	4½" x 7" paper-pieces #6 & #7
	5	3½" x 42"	56	3½" x 3" paper-pieces #2 & #3
	26	3" x 42"	56	3" x 5¼"
			112	3" squares
Fabric C Four-Patch Blocks 1⅓ yards	8	5½" x 42"	56	5½" squares
Fabric D Leaves & Stems ½ yard each of 2 Fabrics	4*	3" x 42"	28*	3" x 5¼"
	2*	1" x 42" *cut for each fabric	14*	1" x 5½"
Fabric E Flower Centers Scraps each of 7 Fabrics	4*	3" squares *cut for each fabric		paper-piece #1
Fabric F Flowers ⅓ yard each of 7 Fabrics	2	4¾" x 42" *cut for each fabric	4*	4¾" x 8" paper-piece #5
			4*	4¾" x 3½" paper-piece #4
First Border ½ yard	8	1½" x 42"		
Second Border ½ yard	8	1¼" x 42"		
Third Border ⅝ yard	9	2" x 42"		
Outside Border 1½ yards	9	5½" x 42"		
Binding ⅞ yard	10	2¾" x 42"		
Backing - 8 yards Batting - 95" x 105"				

Fabric Requirements and Cutting Instructions

Read all instructions before beginning and use ¼"-wide seam allowances throughout. Read Cutting Strips and Pieces on page 124 prior to cutting fabric.

Getting Started

Vivid colors bring a fanciful fresh look to these tulip blocks. Block measures 10½" square (unfinished). Refer to Accurate Seam Allowance on page 124. Whenever possible use Assembly Line Method on page 124. Press seams in direction of arrows.

Making the Four-Patch Blocks

1. Sew lengthwise one 3" x 42" Fabric A strip to one 3" x 42" Fabric B strip as shown to make a strip set. Press seams toward Fabric B. Make nine using assorted Fabric A strips. Cut strip set into 3"-wide segments as shown. Cut one hundred and twelve segments, twelve or thirteen from each strip set.

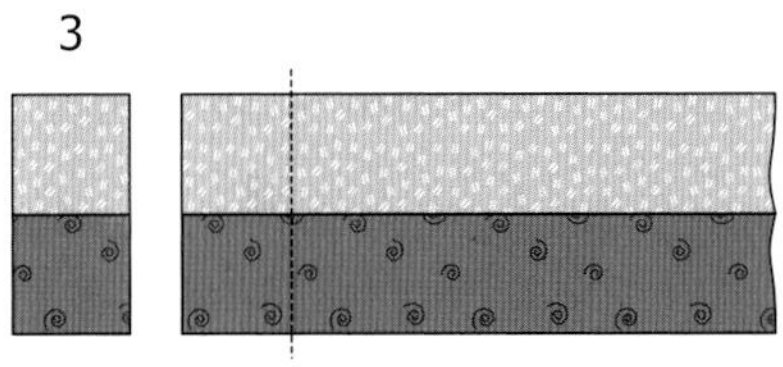

Make 9 using assorted Fabric A strips
Cut a total of 112 segments
(12 or 13 segments from each strip set)

2. Sew two different units from step 1 together alternating fabric as shown. Refer to Twisting Seams on page 124 and press. Make fifty-six assorted units.

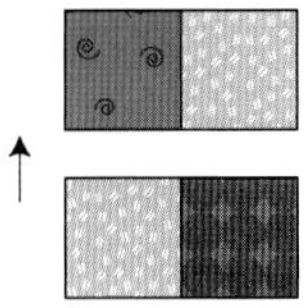

Make 56

3. Sew one unit from step 2 to one 5½" Fabric C square as shown. Press. Make fifty-six.

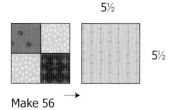

5½

5½

Make 56

4. Sew two units from step 3 together as shown. Twist seams and press. Make twenty-eight. Block measures 10½" square.

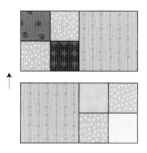

Make 28
Block measures 10½" square

Making the Tulip Blocks

Refer to paper-piecing pattern on page 71. Twenty-eight copies are needed for this project. It is recommended to make a few extra copies. Make all copies from the same copier to avoid distortion. Trim pattern ½" away from outside pattern edge. Units will be trimmed on outside trim line after units are sewn together.

1. Place wrong side of fabric to wrong side of printed pattern centering one 3" Fabric E square over section #1. Pin using a flower-head pin, keeping pin away from stitching lines. If necessary, hold pieces up to light to make sure Fabric E extends past section #1 shape.

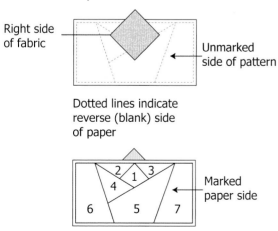

Right side of fabric

Unmarked side of pattern

Dotted lines indicate reverse (blank) side of paper

Marked paper side

2. Using a card stock or file folder to aid in folding paper, fold paper along stitching line between section #1 and #2. Align ruler ¼" from folded paper edge and trim fabric as shown.

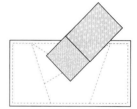

Align ruler ¼" from folded edge.
Trim fabric and unfold paper.

3. Unfold paper, align one 3½" x 3" Fabric B piece on Fabric E cut edge from step 2, right sides together. Pin in place. Once confidence increases with this technique, pieces can be held in place by hand instead of pining. Turn paper printed side up, being careful not to displace fabric on back, sew through all layers along section #1/2 stitching line, using a short stitch length (14"- 20" per inch). Begin and end stitches ¼" beyond stitching line. Turn paper to wrong side, press seams as shown.

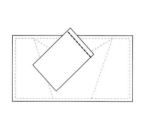

E = 3 x 3
B = 3½ x 3

4. Repeat process to sew one 3½" x 3" Fabric B piece to section #3 as shown.

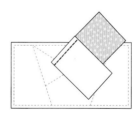

B = 3½ x 3

5. Continue sewing pieces in numerical order. Sew one 4¾" x 3½" Fabric F to section #4 as shown. Sew one 4¾" x 8" Fabric F piece to section #5, and two 4½" x 7" to section #6, and section #7.

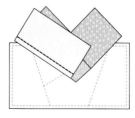
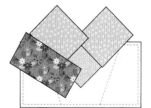

F = 4¾ x 3½

Sunny Tulips Bed Quilt
87½" x 97½"

2001
Tulip Patch
Originally featured in
Floral Inspirations

Don't get me wrong, I still like the colors of the original Tulip Patch quilt (cover of Floral Inspirations ~ 2001), but I LOVE the hot, sunny colors of my updated version. I didn't need to change a thing with the structure of the design, but with these new, fresh colors it transports the quilt out of Grandma's guest room and right into a trendy teen's youthful bedroom digs. When I took a recent look at our Floral Inspirations book, a vivid memory came to mind of a very chilly Maggie Bullock (copy editor) & I standing out on the lawn early in the morning of our photo shoot. We sang every sun-themed song we could think of trying our best to will the sun to peek around the clouds to help us light our outdoor photo set and warm us up a bit!

6. After all sections are sewn, press and trim piece on outside trim line to measure 5½" x 10½".

7. Repeat steps 1-6 to make a total of twenty-eight units, four of each fabric combination.

Make 4

Make 4

Make 4

Make 4

Make 4

Make 4

Make 4

Make 4

8. Refer to Quick Corner Triangles on page 124. Making quick corner triangle units, sew two 3" Fabric B squares to one 3" x 5¼" Fabric D piece as shown. Press. Make twenty-eight, fourteen of each combination.

Fabric B = 3 x 3
Fabric D = 3 x 5¼
Make 14

Fabric B = 3 x 3
Fabric D = 3 x 5¼
Make 14

9. Making quick corner triangle units, sew two 3" Fabric B squares to one 3" x 5¼" Fabric D piece as shown. Press. Make twenty-eight, fourteen of each combination.

Fabric B = 3 x 3
Fabric D = 3 x 5¼
Make 14

Fabric B = 3 x 3
Fabric D = 3 x 5¼
Make 14

10. Sew one 3" x 5¼" Fabric B piece to one unit from step 8 as shown. Press. Make twenty-eight, fourteen of each combination.

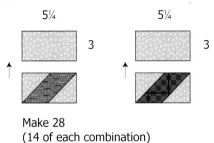

Make 28
(14 of each combination)

11. Sew one 3" x 5¼" Fabric B piece to one unit from step 9 as shown. Press. Make twenty-eight, fourteen of each combination.

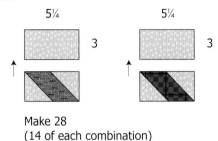

Make 28
(14 of each combination)

12. Sew one 1" x 5½" Fabric D piece between one unit from step 10 and one unit from step 11 together as shown. Note: Match Fabric D pieces throughout each unit. Make twenty-eight, fourteen of each combination.

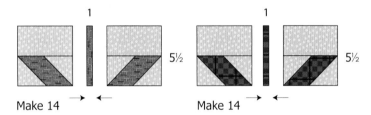

Make 14   Make 14

13. Sew one paper-pieced unit from step 7 to one unit from step 12 as shown. Press. Make twenty-eight in assorted fabric combinations. Block measures 10½" square.

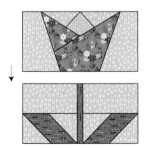

Make 28
(in assorted fabric combinations)
Block measures 10½" square

Assembling the Quilt

1. Refer to photo on page 65 and layout on page 68 to arrange all blocks into rows. Arrange and sew together four Four-Patch blocks and three Tulip Blocks. Press seams toward the Four-Patch blocks Make four and label these rows 1, 3, 5, and 7.

2. Arrange and sew together four Tulip Blocks and three Four-Patch blocks as shown. Press seams toward the Four-Patch blocks. Make four and label these rows 2, 4, 6, and 8.

3. Arrange rows in numerical orders and sew rows together. Press.

Adding the Borders

1. Refer to Adding the Borders on page 125. Sew 1½" x 42" First Border strips together end-to-end to make one continuous 1½"-wide First Border strip. Measure quilt through center from side to side. Cut two 1½"-wide First Border strips to this measurement. Sew to top and bottom of quilt. Press seams toward border.

2. Measure quilt through center from top to bottom including borders just added. Cut two 1½"-wide First Border strips to this measurement. Sew to sides of quilt. Press.

3. Refer to steps 1 and 2 to join, measure, trim, and sew 1¼"-wide Second Border, 2"-wide Third Border, and 5½"-wide Outside Border strips to top, bottom, and sides of quilt. Press.

Layering and Finishing

1. Cut backing crosswise into three equal pieces. Sew pieces together lengthwise to make one 96" x 120" (approximate) backing piece. Press and trim to 96" x 105".

2. Referring to Layering the Quilt on page 125, arrange and baste backing, batting, and top together. Hand or machine quilt as desired.

3. Refer to Binding the Quilt on page 125. Sew 2¾" x 42" binding strips end-to-end to make one continuous 2¾"-wide binding strip. Bind quilt to finish.

Sunny Tulips Bed Quilt

28 copies are needed for this project. It is recommended to make a few extra copies. Compare copy to the original. Copy should measure 5½" x 10½". Adjust copier setting if it varies. Trim pattern ½" larger than outside pattern edge. Piece will be trimmed to measure 5½" x 10½" after all fabrics has been sewn to pattern.

7

3

1

5

2

4

6

Outside Trim Line

Permission is granted by Debbie Mumm® to copy page 71 to successfully complete the Sunny Tulips Bed Quilt.

Fantasy Flowers

bed ■ quilt

Fantasy Flowers Bed Quilt Finished Size: 89½" x 115"	FIRST CUT		SECOND CUT	
	Number of Strips or Pieces	Dimensions	Number of Pieces	Dimensions
Fabric A Background Dark 5¾ yards	3	26¾" x 42"	3	26¾" squares* *cut twice diagonally
	1	13 ⅝ " x 42"	2	13 ⅝ " squares** **cut once diagonally
	16	4½" x 42"	12	4½" x 18½"
			12	4½" x 10½"
			48	4½" squares
	8	2½" x 42"	120	2½" squares
	8	1½" x 42"	192	1½" squares
Fabric B Large & Small Light Hearts	2*	5½" x 42"	12*	5½" x 4½"
Fabric C Large & Small Dark Hearts	3*	3½" x 42"	10*	3½" squares
Fabric F Large & Small Dark Hearts			20*	3½" x 2½"
Fabric G Large & Small Light Hearts			6*	2½" squares
Fabric H Large & Small Dark Hearts	1*	1½" x 42"	24*	1½" squares
Fabric I Large & Small Light Hearts ¾ yard each of 6 Fabrics		*cut for each fabric (B, C, F, G, H & I)		
Fabric D Large & Small Light Hearts	2*	5½" x 42"	12*	5½" x 4½"
Fabric E Large & Small Dark Hearts	2*	3½" x 42"	6*	3½" squares
			12*	3½" x 2½"
			6*	2½" squares
⅝ yard each of 2 Fabrics	1*	1½" x 42" *cut for each fabric (D & E)	24*	1½" squares
First Border ½ yard	10	1½" x 42"		
Second Border ⅔ yard	10	2" x 42"		
Outside Border 1¼ yards	10	4" x 42"		
Binding 1 yard	11	2¾" x 42"		
Backing - 10¼ yards Batting - 98" x 123"				

Fabric Requirements and Cutting Instructions

Read all instructions before beginning and use ¼"-wide seam allowances throughout. Read Cutting Strips and Pieces on page 124 prior to cutting fabric.

Getting Started

These flowers, with their heart-shaped petals, look great in any fabric color combination. Block measures 18½" square (unfinished). Refer to Accurate Seam Allowance on page 124. Whenever possible use Assembly Line Method on page 124. Press seams in direction of arrows.

Making the Large Flower Blocks

1. Refer to Quick Corner Triangles on page 124. Making quick corner triangle units, sew one 1½" square and one 2½" Fabric A square to one 5½" x 4½" Fabric B piece as shown. Press. Make six. Sew one 1½" and one 2½" Fabric A squares to one 5½" x 4½" Fabric C piece. Press. Make six.

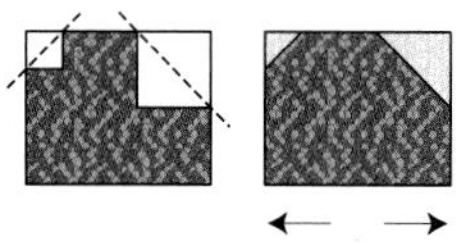

Fabric A = 1½ x 1½
2½ x 2½
Fabric B = 5½ x 4½
Make 6

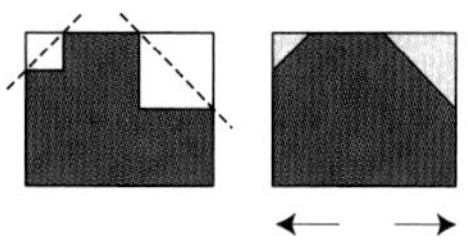

Fabric A = 1½ x 1½
2½ x 2½
Fabric C = 5½ x 4½
Make 6

Fantasy Flowers Bed Quilt
89½" x 115"

3. Making quick corner triangle units, sew two 1½" Fabric B squares to one 3½" x 2½" Fabric F piece. Press. Make twelve. Sew two 1½" Fabric C squares to one 3½" x 2½" Fabric G piece. Press. Make twelve.

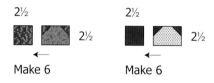

Fabric B = 1½ x 1½   Fabric C = 1½ x 1½
Fabric F = 3½ x 2½   Fabric G = 3½ x 2½
Make 12   Make 12

4. Sew one 2½" Fabric B square to one B/F unit from step 3 as shown. Press. Make six. Sew one 2½" Fabric C square to one C/G unit from step 3. Press. Make six.

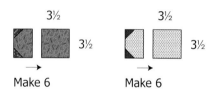

Make 6   Make 6

5. Sew one B/F unit from step 3 to one 3½" Fabric F square as shown. Press. Make six. Sew one C/G unit from step 3 to one 3½" Fabric C square. Press. Make six.

Make 6   Make 6

6. Sew one unit from step 4 to one matching unit from step 5 as shown. Press. Make twelve, six of each combination.

Make 6   Make 6

2. Making quick corner triangle units, sew one 2½" and one 1½" Fabric A squares to one 5½" x 4½" Fabric B piece as shown. Note: Square placement varies from step 1. Press. Make six. Sew one 2½" and one 1½" Fabric A squares to one 5½" x 4½" Fabric C piece. Press. Make six.

Fabric A = 2½ x 2½   Fabric A = 2½ x 2½
           1½ x 1½   1½ x 1½
Fabric B = 5½ x 4½   Fabric C = 5½ x 4½
Make 6   Make 6

7. Sew one 4½" Fabric A square to one unit from step 1 as shown. Press. Make twelve, six of each combination.

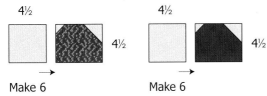

Make 6   Make 6

8. Sew one unit from step 2 to one matching unit from step 6 as shown. Press. Make twelve, six of each combination.

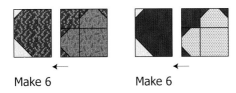

Make 6   Make 6

9. Sew one unit from step 7 to one matching unit from step 8 as shown. Press. Make twelve, six of each combination.

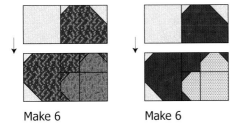

Make 6   Make 6

10. Sew two units from step 9, one of each fabric combination as shown. Press. Make six.

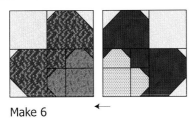

Make 6

11. Sew two units from step 10 together as shown. Make three and label Block 1. Block measures 18½" square.

Block 1

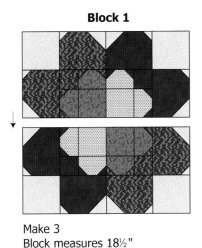

Make 3
Block measures 18½"

Some of my staff thought I was a little too far out-of-the-box when I used the color brown for flower petals in the remake of this 2002 Hearts & Flowers quilt from our title, Quilting Through the Year. I reminded them, as I often do...."Remember, we are living in a fantasy world here ~ Don't worry about reality." That has always been my motto when it comes to creating art. We get enough reality as it is. My goal with this quilt was to create a modern/ vintage look (if there is such a thing!) with the combination of the design and color story. Sometimes I enjoy creating quilts with layers of meaning and other times - I just do what appeals to me whether is makes much sense or not. That's the fun of designing.

2002
Hearts & Flowers
Originally featured in
Quilting Through
the Years

12. Repeat steps 1-11 to make three of Block 2 using Fabrics A, D, E, H, and I; three of Block 3 using Fabrics A, F, G, D, E; and three of Block 4 using Fabrics A, H, I, C, B.

Block 2   **Block 3**

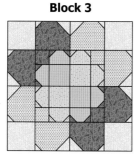

Make 3
(Fabrics A/D/E/H/I)
Block measures 18½"

Make 3
(Fabrics A/F/G/D/E)
Block measures 18½"

Block 4

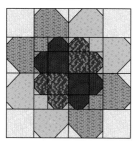

Make 3
(Fabrics A/H/I/C/B)
Block measures 18½"

Making the Small Flower Blocks

1. Refer to Quick Corner Triangles on page 124. Making quick corner triangle units, sew two 1½" Fabric A squares to one 3½" x 2½" Fabric H piece as shown. Press. Make eight. Sew two 1½" Fabric A squares to one 3½" x 2½" Fabric I piece. Press. Make eight.

Fabric A = 1½ x 1½   Fabric A = 1½ x 1½
Fabric H = 3½ x 2½   Fabric I = 3½ x 2½
Make 8   Make 8

2. Sew one 2½" Fabric A square to one unit from step 1 as shown. Press. Make eight, four of each combination.

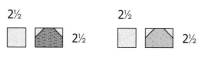

2½   2½

              2½   2½

Make 4   Make 4

3. Sew one matching unit from step 1 to one 3½" Fabric H square as shown. Press. Make four. Sew one matching unit from step 1 to one 3½" Fabric I square as shown. Press. Make four.

3½   3½

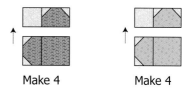

3½   3½

Make 4   Make 4

4. Sew one unit from step 2 to one matching unit from step 3 as shown. Press. Make eight, four of each combination.

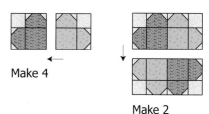

Make 4   Make 4

5. Sew together two units from step 4, one of each fabric combination as shown. Press. Make four. Sew two of these units together as shown. Press. Make two.

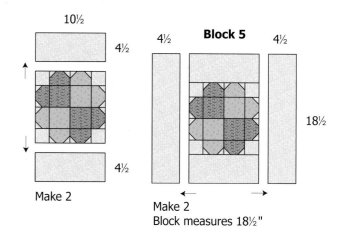

Make 4

Make 2

6. Sew one unit from step 5 between two 4½" x 10½" Fabric A pieces. Press. Sew this unit between two 4½" x 18½" Fabric A pieces. Press. Make two and label Block 5. Block measures 18½" square.

10½

4½   4½   **Block 5**   4½

                                        18½

Make 2

Make 2
Block measures 18½"

7. Repeat steps 1-6 to make two of Block 6 using fabrics A, B, and C; and two of Block 7 using fabrics A, G, and F.

Block 6   **Block 7**

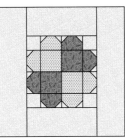

Make 2
(Fabrics A/B/C)
Block measures 18½"

Make 2
(Fabrics A/G/F)
Block measures 18½"

Assembling the Quilt

1. Refer to photo on page 73, layout on page 74, and diagram below to arrange blocks and side and corner triangles in diagonal rows prior to sewing. There will be two side-setting triangles left over.

2. Sew blocks and side triangles into rows as shown. Press seams away from Large Flower blocks.

3. Sew rows together. Press seams in one direction. Sew corner triangles to quilt.

Adding the Borders

1. Refer to Adding the Borders on page 126. Sew 1½" x 42" First Border strips together end-to-end to make one continuous 1½"-wide First Border strip. Measure quilt through center from side to side. Cut two 1½"-wide First Border strips to this measurement. Sew to top and bottom of quilt. Press seams toward border.

2. Measure quilt through center from top to bottom including borders just added. Cut two 1½"-wide First Border strips to this measurement. Sew to sides of quilt. Press.

3. Refer to steps 1 and 2 to join, measure, trim, and sew 2"-wide Second Border strips and 4"-wide Outside Border strips to top, bottom, and sides of quilt. Press.

Layering and Finishing

1. Cut backing crosswise into three equal pieces. Sew pieces together lengthwise to make one 120" x 123" (approximate) backing piece. Press.

2. Referring to Layering the Quilt on page 126, arrange and baste backing, batting, and top together. Hand or machine quilt as desired.

3. Refer to Binding the Quilt on page 126. Sew 2¾" x 42" binding strips end-to-end to make one continuous 2¾"-wide binding strip. Bind quilt to finish.

Colorful Fall Leaves

wall ▪ quilt

Colorful Fall Leaves Wall Quilt Finished Size: 37" x 37"	FIRST CUT		SECOND CUT	
	Number of Strips or Pieces	Dimensions	Number of Pieces	Dimensions
Fabric A Light Background & Leaves ⅓ yard each of 8 Fabrics	2*	9" squares *cut for each fabric (1 for block background & 1 for leaf appliqués)		
Fabric B Dark Background & Leaves ⅓ yard each of 8 Fabrics	2*	9" squares *cut for each fabric (1 for block background & 1 for leaf appliqués)		
First Border ⅙ yard	4	1" x 42"	2 2	1" x 33½" 1" x 32½"
Outside Border ⅓ yard	4	2" x 42"	2 2	2" x 36½" 2" x 33½"
Binding ⅜ yard	4	2¾" x 42"		
Backing - 1⅛ yards Batting - 41" x 41" Lightweight Fusible Web - 2 yards				

Fabric Requirements and Cutting Instructions

Read all instructions before beginning and use ¼"-wide seam allowances throughout. Read Cutting Strips and Pieces on page 124 prior to cutting fabric.

Getting Started

Bring the beautiful colors of fall to your home with these multicolored whirling leaves. Block measures 8½" square (unfinished). Refer to Accurate Seam Allowance on page 124. Whenever possible use Assembly Line Method on page 124. Press seams in direction of arrows.

Making the Block

Refer to appliqué instructions on page 125. Our instructions are for Quick-Fuse Appliqué, but if you prefer hand appliqué, reverse patterns and add ¼"-wide seam allowances.

1. Draw a diagonal line on wrong side of one 9" Fabric A square. Place marked square and one 9" Fabric B square right sides together. Sew scant ¼" away from drawn line on both sides to make half-square triangles as shown. Make eight, one of each fabric combination. Cut on drawn line and press. Square unit to 8½". This will make sixteen half-square triangle units, two of each fabric combination.

Fabric A = 9 x 9
Fabric B = 9 x 9
Make 8
(1 of each fabric combination)

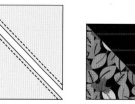

Square to 8½"
Make 16
(2 of each fabric combination)
Half-square Triangle Units

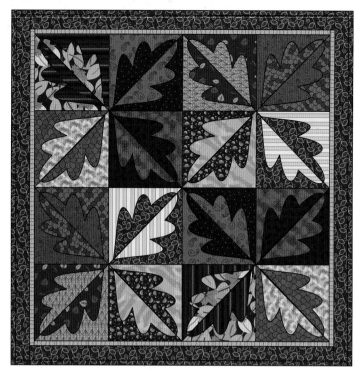

Colorful Fall Leaves Wall Quilt
37" x 37"

2. Use patterns on page 81 to trace thirty-two, sixteen along outside edge including dashed line and sixteen reversed tracing solid lines only, leaf pattern on paper side of fusible web. Use appropriate fabrics to prepare all appliqués for fusing. Note: Use extra Fabric A and B squares to make two leaves of each fabric. Each block consists of the same fabric for background and leaves placing light leaf on dark background and dark leaf on light background. Refer to photo and layout to determine which leaf pattern to use for each fabric. Reminder: Patterns are reversed for quick-fused appliqués, so finished appliqués will be in the opposite position. Match leaf and background stripe direction for directional blocks.

3. Use an appliqué-pressing sheet to fuse two partial leaves together to make a whole leaf. Make sixteen, two of each combination. If appliqué pressing sheet is not available then delete this step. Position appliqués carefully on each block in next step prior to fusing.

Fuse two leaf halves together overlapping pieces as shown.

3. Refer to photo on page 79 and layout to position and fuse appliqués to each quilt block. Finish appliqué edges with machine satin stitch or other decorative stitching as desired.

Assembling and Adding the Borders

1. Sew two blocks together as shown. Press. Make eight, two of each fabric combination. Sew two different units together as shown. Press. Make four, two of each fabric combination. Refer to Twisting Seams on page 124 and press.

Make 8 →
(2 of each fabric combination)

Make 4
(2 of each fabric combination)

2. Referring to photo on page 79 and layout, sew two blocks together from step 1 to make a row. Make two. Press. Sew rows together and press.

3. Refer to Adding the Borders on page 126. Sew two 1" x 32½" First Border strips to top and bottom of quilt. Press seams toward border.

4. Sew two 1" x 33½" First Border strips to sides of quilt. Press seams toward border.

5. Sew two 2" x 33½" Outside Border strips to top and bottom of quilt. Press seams toward border.

6. Sew two 2" x 36½" Outside Border strips to sides of quilt. Press seams toward border.

Layering and Finishing

1. Referring to Layering the Quilt on page 126, arrange and baste backing, batting, and top together. Hand or machine quilt as desired.

2. Refer to Binding the Quilt on page 126. Use 2¾"-wide binding strips to bind quilt.

Colorful Fall Leaves Wall Quilt

Patterns are reversed for use with Quick-Fuse Appliqué (page 125)

Tracing Line ——————————
Tracing Line - - - - - - - - - - - -
(will be hidden behind other fabrics)

Make 16
Tracing along outside edge including dashed line.

Make 16 reversed
Tracing solid lines only.

Full Pattern includes dash line.

Reversed solid lines only

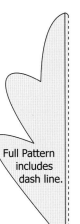

I really like wall quilts because you can create and complete them so much faster than a bed quilt. Plus, you save a few dollars on supplies. My inspiration for this wall quilt was a bed size quilt called "Blowing in the Wind" (which also tells you that I'm a folk music fan). I love the dramatic impact created by dividing the leaf in half with contrasting fabrics–you accomplish a strong light and dark play this way. And, to make it even faster, I changed the design from pieced to appliqué. Also notice the echo quilting around the leaf shapes – a very effective treatment to create nice visual texture.

2003
Blowing in the Wind
Originally featured in Quilts from a Gardener's Journal

Happy Harvest

wall ▪ banner

Happy Harvest Wall Banner Finished Size: 18" x 21"	FIRST CUT		SECOND CUT	
	Number of Strips or Pieces	Dimensions	Number of Pieces	Dimensions
Fabric A Leaf Background ⅛ yard each of 4 Fabrics	1*	1½" x 42" *cut for each fabric	12*	1½" squares
Fabric B Leaves ⅛ yard each of 4 Fabrics	1*	1½" x 42" *cut for each fabric	2* 2* 4*	1½" x 3½" 1½" x 2½" 1½" squares
Fabric C Pumpkin Background ⅛ yard	1	2½" x 42"	1 1 6	2½" x 12½" 1½" x 3½" 1½" squares
Fabric D Medium Pumpkin Scrap	1	4½" x 5½"		
Fabric E Large Pumpkin Scrap	1	5½" square		
Fabric F Small Pumpkin Scrap	1	3½" x 4½"		
Fabric G Checkerboard Dark ⅛ yard	1	1½" x 42"	2	1½" x 12"
Fabric H Checkerboard Light Scrap each of 2 Fabrics	1*	1½" x 12" *cut for each fabric		
First Border ⅛ yard	2	1" x 42"	2 2	1" x 16½" 1" x 12½"
Second Border ⅛ yard	2	1" x 42"	2 2	1" x 17½" 1" x 13½"
Outside Border ⅙ yard	2	2" x 42"	2 2	2" x 20½" 2" x 14½"
Binding ¼ yard	2	2¾" x 42"		

Appliqué Stems - Assorted scraps
Backing - ⅝ yard
Batting - 22" x 25"
Lightweight Fusible Web - Scraps
**If using Fabric A or B for checkerboard light fabrics, no additional fabric is needed.

Fabric Requirements and Cutting Instructions

Read all instructions before beginning and use ¼"-wide seam allowances throughout. Read Cutting Strips and Pieces on page 124 prior to cutting fabric.

Getting Started

Crisp fall air brings the changing of the season with its colorful leaves and pumpkin patches. Leaf Block measures 3½" square (unfinished). Refer to Accurate Seam Allowance on page 124. Whenever possible use Assembly Line Method on page 124. Press seams in direction of arrows.

Making the Quilt

1. Refer to Quick Corner Triangles on page 124. Making a quick corner triangle unit, sew one 1½" Fabric A square to one 1½" Fabric B square as shown. Press. Make four.

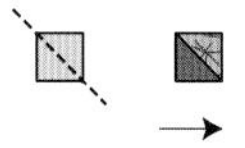

Fabric A = 1½ x 1½
Fabric B = 1½ x 1½
Make 4

2. Sew one 1½" Fabric A square to two units from step 1 as shown. Press. Make two.

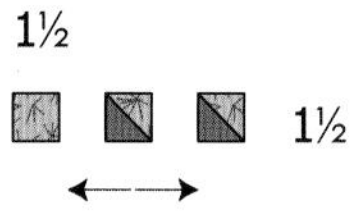

Make 2

3. Making a quick corner triangle unit, sew one 1½" Fabric A square to one 1½" x 3½" Fabric B piece as shown. Press. Make two.

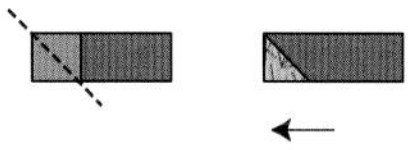

Fabric A = 1½ x 1½
Fabric B = 1½ x 3½
Make 2

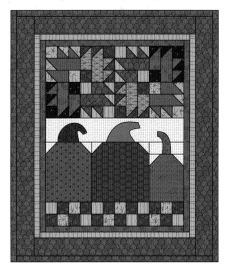

Happy Harvest Wall Banner
18" x 21"

7. Sew two different leaf blocks together. Press. Make four, two of each combination.

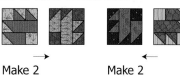

Make 2   Make 2

8. Sew two units from step 7, one of each combination, together as shown. Press. Make two. Sew units together as shown. Press.

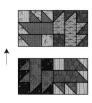

Make 2

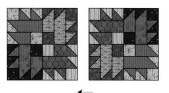

4. Making a quick corner triangle unit, sew one 1½" Fabric A square to one 1½" x 2½" Fabric B piece as shown. Press. Sew this unit to one 1½" Fabric A square. Press.

Fabric A = 1½ x 1½
Fabric B = 1½ x 2½
Make 2

1½

1½

Make 2

9. Making quick corner triangle units, sew two 1½" Fabric C squares to one 4½" x 5½" Fabric D piece as shown. Press.

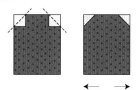

Fabric C = 1½ x 1½
Fabric D = 4½ x 5½

5. Arrange and sew together one unit from step 2, one unit from step 3 and one unit from step 4 as shown. Press. Make two leaf blocks. Block measures 3½" square.

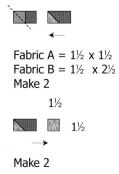

Make 2
Block measures 3½" square

10. Making quick corner triangle units, sew two 1½" Fabric C squares to one 5½" Fabric E square as shown. Press.

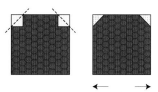

Fabric C = 1½ x 1½
Fabric E = 5½ x 5½

6. Repeat step 1-5 to sew six additional leaf blocks, two of each fabric combination.

Make 2

Make 2   Make 2

1997
Happy Harvest
Originally featured in
Autumn & Winter
Seasonal Sampler

I've always had a soft spot for this sweet little harvest banner with these personality-filled pumpkins. When I designed this wall quilt for my 1997 release, Autumn & Winter Seasonal Sampler, my design was uniquely asymmetrical. So for my updated version, I balanced the design to make it more traditionally symmetrical and simpler looking–following a current trend for clean and simple design. Luckily, the traditional harvest palette is still popular today.

11. Making quick corner triangle units, sew two 1½" Fabric C squares to one 3½" x 4½" Fabric F piece as shown. Press. Sew this unit to one 1½" x 3½" Fabric C piece as shown.

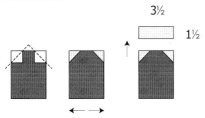

Fabric C = 1½ x 1½
Fabric F = 3½ x 4½

12. Sew unit from step 10 between units from step 9 and 11 as shown. Press.

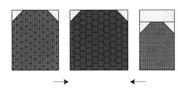

13. Sew lengthwise one 1½" x 12" Fabric H piece to one 1½" x 12" Fabric G piece as shown to make a strip set. Press seams toward Fabric H. Make second strip set using remaining 1½" Fabric H and G pieces. Press toward Fabric H. Cut each strip set into six 1½"-wide segments, for a total of twelve segments, as shown.

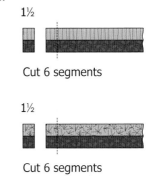

14. Arrange and sew together twelve units from step 13 alternating Fabric G as shown. Press.

15. Arrange and sew together unit from step 8, one 2½" x 12½" Fabric C piece, unit from step 12 and unit from step 14 as shown. Press.

12½

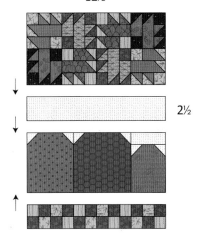

2½

Adding the Appliqués
Refer to appliqué instructions on page 125. Our instructions are for Quick-Fuse Appliqué, but if you prefer hand appliqué, reverse patterns and add ¼"-wide seam allowances.

1. Use patterns on this page to trace pumpkin stems on paper side of fusible web. Use appropriate fabrics to prepare all appliqués for fusing.

2. Refer to photo on page 83 and layout on page 84 to position and fuse appliqués to top of pumpkins. Finish appliqué edges with machine satin stitch or other decorative stitching as desired.

Adding the Borders

1. Refer to Adding the Borders on page 126. Sew two 1" x 12½" First Border strips to top and bottom of quilt. Press seams toward border. Sew two 1" x 16½" First Border strips to sides of quilt. Press.

2. Sew two 1" x 13½" Second Border strips to top and bottom of quilt. Press seams toward border just sewn. Sew two 1" x 17½" Second Border strips to sides of quilt. Press.

3. Sew two 2" x 14½" Outside Border strips to top and bottom of quilt. Press seams toward border. Sew two 2" x 20½" Outside Border strips to sides of quilt. Press.

Layering and Finishing

1. Referring to Layering the Quilt on page 126, arrange and baste backing, batting, and top together. Hand or machine quilt as desired.

2. Refer to Binding the Quilt on page 126. Use 2¾"-wide binding strips to bind quilt.

**Happy Harvest
Wall Banner**
Patterns are reversed for use with
Quick -Fuse Appliqué (page 125)
Tracing Line _____

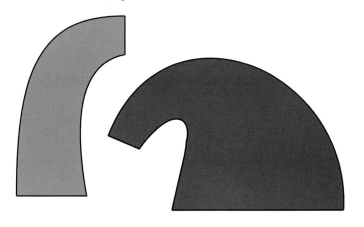

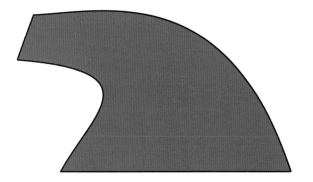

Prairie Quail

lap ▪ quilt

Prairie Quail Lap Quilt Finished Size: 42" x 42"	FIRST CUT		SECOND CUT	
	Number of Strips or Pieces	Dimensions	Number of Pieces	Dimensions
Fabric A Block 1 Assorted scraps	20	6½" squares (In assorted fabrics)		
Fabric B Block Accent ¼ yard each of 4 Fabrics	1*	4½" x 42" *cut for each fabric	4*	4½" squares Note: We used four different fabrics cutting eight squares from one.
Fabric C Block 2 Background ⅓ yard	1	8½" x 42"	4	8½" squares
Fabric D Block 2 First Border ⅓ yard	5	1½" x 42"	8 8	1½" x 10½" 1½" x 8½"
Fabric E Block 2 Second Border ⅓ yard	6	1½" x 42"	8 8	1½" x 12½" 1½" x 10½"
Fabric F Block 2 Accent Border ⅓ yard	2	4½" x 42"	16	4½" squares
First & Third Border ⅜ yard	4 4	1½" x 42" 1" x 42"	2 2 2 2	1½" x 38½" 1½" x 36½" 1" x 40½" 1" x 39½"
Second Border ⅙ yard	4	1" x 42"	2 2	1" x 39½" 1" x 38½"
Outside Border ¼ yard	4	1" x 42"	2 2	1" x 41½" 1" x 40½"
Binding ½ yard	5	2¾" x 42"		
Appliqué - Assorted wool scraps Backing - 1⅓ yards (Fabric must measure 45"-wide) Batting - 45" x 45" ⅛" Buttons - 4 for eyes Lightweight Fusible Web - ½ yard				

Fabric Requirements and Cutting Instructions

Read all instructions before beginning and use ¼"-wide seam allowances throughout. Read Cutting Strips and Pieces on page 124 prior to cutting fabric.

Getting Started

Colorful quail scurry across this beautiful autumn quilt. Block measures 12½" square (unfinished). Refer to Accurate Seam Allowance on page 124. Whenever possible use Assembly Line Method on page 124. Press seams in direction of arrows.

Making Block 1

Note: Our quilt uses thirteen different Fabric A fabrics, doubles of some were cut to make a total of twenty 6½" squares.

1. Sew two different 6½" Fabric A squares together. Press. Make ten in assorted combinations.

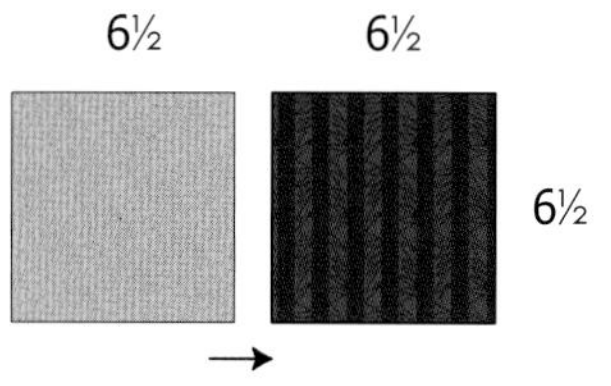

Make 10
(in assorted combinations)

2. Sew two units from step 1 together as shown. Refer to Twisting Seams on page 124 and press. Make five.

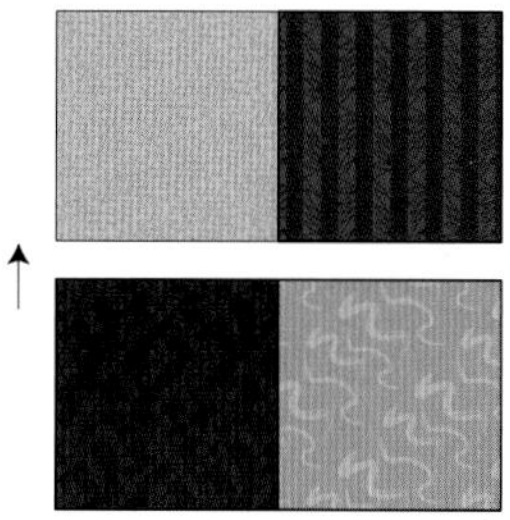

Make 5
(in assorted combinations)

3. Refer to Quick Corner Triangles on page 124. Making quick corner triangle units, sew four matching 4½" Fabric B squares to one unit from step 2 as shown. Press. Make five and label Block 1. Block measures 12½" square.

Block 1

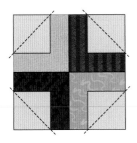 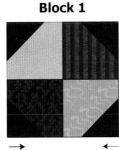

Fabric B = 4½ x 4½
Unit from step 2
Make 5

Block measures 12½" square

Making Block 2

1. Sew one 8½" Fabric C square between two 1½" x 8½" Fabric D pieces. Press seams toward Fabric D. Sew this unit between two 1½" x 10½" Fabric D pieces as shown. Press. Make four.

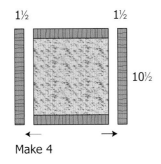

1½   1½

10½

Make 4

2. Sew one unit from step 1 between two 1½" x 10½" Fabric E pieces. Press seams toward Fabric E. Sew this unit between two 1½" x 12½" Fabric E pieces as shown. Press. Make four.

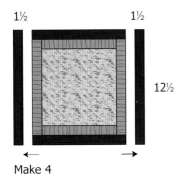

1½   1½

12½

Make 4

I hope it's okay to say this — I just love this quilt! I live in an area called Five Mile Prairie which is populated with coveys of plump quail and I find these handsome birds very inspirational for quilts and artwork. I referenced two previous designs as inspiration to create this new quail quilt. A long-standing staff favorite called Woodland Beauty was featured on the cover of Cozy Northwest Christmas (circa 2003) and Autumn Glory from 2002's Quilting Through the Year somehow came together for this new interpretation. The appliquéd, chubby, quail are particularly rich in color thanks to sourcing my bin of luscious wool scraps.

2003 Woodland Beauty
Originally featured in Cozy Northwest Christmas

2002 Autumn Glory
Originally featured in Quilting Through the Year

Prairie Quail Lap Quilt
42" x 42"

Adding the Appliqués
Refer to appliqué instructions on page 125. Our instructions are for Quick-Fuse Appliqué, but if you prefer hand appliqué, reverse patterns and add ¼"-wide seam allowances.

1. Use patterns on page 91 to trace four quails on paper side of fusible web. Use appropriate fabrics to prepare all appliqués for fusing.

2. Refer to photo on page 87 and layout to position and fuse appliqués to Block 2. Finish appliqué edges with machine satin stitch or other decorative stitching as desired.

Assembling

1. Referring to photo on page 87 and layout, sew one Block 2 between two of Block 1. Press seams toward Block 1. Make two.

2. Sew one Block 1 between two of Block 2. Press seams toward Block 1.

3. Referring to photo on page 87 and layout, sew row from step 2 between rows from step 1. Press.

3. Refer to Quick Corner Triangles on page 124. Making quick corner triangle units, sew four 4½" Fabric F squares to one unit from step 2 as shown. Press. Make four and label Block 2. Block measures 12½" square.

Block 2

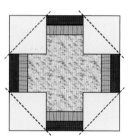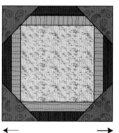

Fabric F = 4½ x 4½
Unit from step 2
Make 4

Block measures 12½" square

Adding the Borders
Note: If fabric width measures less than 42", cut extra border strips and sew together end-to-end, and cut size indicated in chart.

1. Refer to Adding the Borders on page 126. Sew 1½" x 36½" First Border strips to top and bottom of quilt. Press seams toward border. Sew 1½" x 38½" First Border strips to sides of quilt. Press.

2. Sew 1" x 38½" Second Border strips to top and bottom of quilt. Press seams toward border just sewn. Sew 1" x 39½" Second Border strips to sides. Press.

3. Sew 1" x 39½" Third Border strips to top and bottom of quilt. Press seams toward border just sewn. Sew 1" x 40½" Third Border strips to sides. Press.

4. Sew 1" x 40½" Outside Border strips to top and bottom of quilt. Press seams toward border just sewn. Press. Sew 1" x 41½" Outside Border strips to sides. Press.

Tips for Felting Wool

1. Wet wool fabric or WoolFelt™ with hot water. Do not mix colors as dyes may run.

2. Blot wool with a dry towel and place both towel and wool in dryer on high heat until thoroughly dry. The result is a thicker, fuller fabric that will give added texture to the wool. Pressing felted wool is not recommended, as it will flatten the texture. Most wools will shrink 15-30% when felted, adjust yardage accordingly.

**Prairie Quail
Lap Quilt**

Patterns are reversed for use with Quick-Fuse Appliqué (page 125)

Tracing Line ——————
Tracing Line - - - - - - - - - - - - - - -
(will be hidden behind other fabrics)

Layering and Finishing

1. Referring to Layering the Quilt on page 126, arrange and baste backing, batting, and top together. Hand or machine quilt as desired.

2. Refer to Binding the Quilt on page 126. Use 2¾"-wide binding strips to bind quilt.

3. Sew ⅛ " buttons to quail for eyes.

Happy Holidays Penguin

wall ■ banner

Happy Holidays Penguin Wall Banner Finished Size: 16" x 29"	FIRST CUT		SECOND CUT	
	Number of Strips or Pieces	Dimensions	Number of Pieces	Dimensions
Fabric A Background ⅜ yard	1	6½" x 42"	1	6½" x 15½"
	1	3½" x 42"	2	3½" x 10½"
			2	3½" squares
			2	2½" squares
			1	2" x 8½"
	1	1" x 42"	2	1" x 16½"
Fabric B Penguin ¼ yard	1	3½" x 42"	2	3½" x 6½"
			1	2½" x 8½"
	1	1½" x 42"	2	1½" x 7"
			6	1½" squares
Fabric C Penguin Face & Chest ¼ yard	1	6½" x 42"	1	6½" x 8½"
			1	6½" x 6"
			2	1½" x 3½"
Fabric D Banner Accent ⅙ yard	1	3½" x 42"	2	3½" x 15½"
Scarf ⅙ yard	1	4½" x 42"	2	4½" x 16"
Binding ½ yard	1	3½" x 42"	3	3½" x 7½"
	3	2¾" x 42"		

Appliqué Letters - ⅛ yard
Appliqués - Assorted scraps
Earmuff Wire - ¼ yard
Cut one 1½" x 16" Bias strip
Backing - ⅝ yard
Batting - 20" x 33"
Lightweight Fusible Web - ½ yard

Fabric Requirements and Cutting Instructions

Read all instructions before beginning and use ¼"-wide seam allowances throughout. Read Cutting Strips and Pieces on page 124 prior to cutting fabric. Note: Our quilt used Berber for earmuff and one small snowflake appliqué.

Getting Started

Dressed in earmuffs and scarf, this stylish penguin warmly greets holiday quests. Refer to Accurate Seam Allowance on page 124. Whenever possible use Assembly Line Method on page 124. Press seams in direction of arrows.

Making the Banner

1. Refer to Quick Corner Triangles on page 124. Making quick corner triangle units, sew two 2½" Fabric A squares to one 2½" x 8½" Fabric B piece as shown. Press. Sew one 2" x 8½" Fabric A piece to this unit as shown. Press.

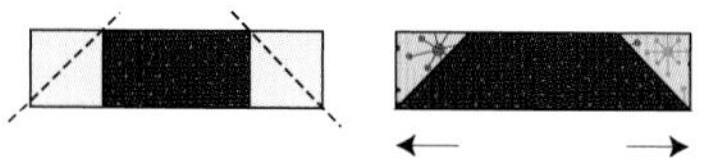

Fabric A = 2½ x 2½
Fabric B = 2½ x 8½

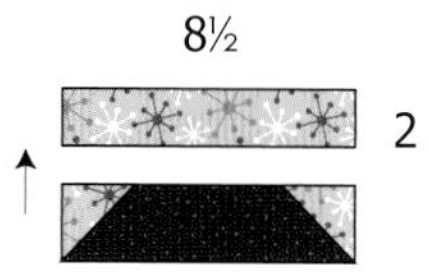

2. Making quick corner triangle units, sew two 1½" Fabric B squares to one 1½" x 3½" Fabric C piece as shown. Press. Make two. Sew these two units together. Press.

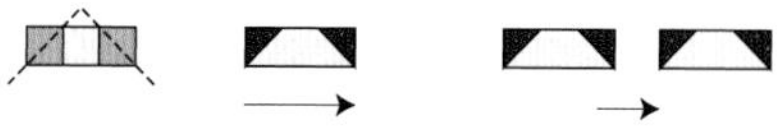

Fabric B = 1½ x 1½
Fabric C = 1½ x 3½
Make 2

3. Sew unit from step 2 to one 6½" x 6" Fabric C piece as shown. Press.

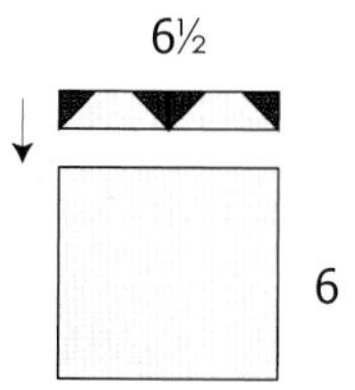

4. Sew unit from step 3 between two 1½" x 7" Fabric B pieces as shown. Press.

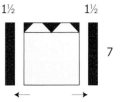

5. Sew unit from step 4 between two 3½" x 10½" Fabric A pieces as shown. Press.

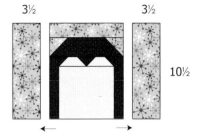

6. Making quick corner triangle units, sew two 1½" Fabric B squares to one 6½" x 8½" Fabric C piece as shown. Press.

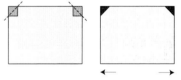

Fabric B = 1½ x 1½
Fabric C = 8½ x 6½

7. Making a quick corner triangle unit sew one 3½" Fabric A square to one 3½" x 6½" Fabric B piece as shown. Press. Make two, one of each variation.

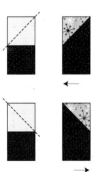

Fabric A = 3½ x 3½
Fabric B = 3½ x 6½
Make 2
(1 of each variation)

**Happy Holidays Penguin
Wall Banner**
16" x 29"

10. Arrange and sew together two 3½" x 15½" Fabric D strips, unit from step 9, and one 6½" x 15½" Fabric A piece as shown. Press.

15½

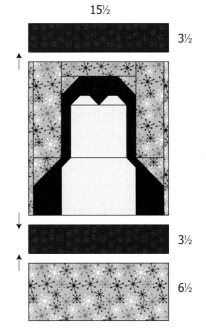

3½

3½

6½

Adding the Appliqués
Refer to appliqué instructions on page 125. Our instructions are for Quick-Fuse Appliqué, but if you prefer hand appliqué, reverse patterns and add ¼"-wide seam allowances. Note: We used Berber for the earmuff and the smaller "Holiday" snowflake.

1. To make earmuff wire, fold 1½" x 20" bias strip in half lengthwise with wrong sides together. Sew ¼" seam on edge opposite fold. Trim seam to ⅛". Press strip flat with seam in center back. Hand or machine blind hem stitch strip forming an arch, from one earmuff to the other, centering in place.

2. Use patterns on page 96 to trace three small snowflakes, one large snowflake, letters, earmuff, and penguin's beak and eyes on paper side of fusible web. Use appropriate fabrics to prepare all appliqués for fusing.

3. Refer to photo on page 93 and layout to position and fuse appliqués to quilt. Finish appliqué edges with machine satin stitch or other decorative stitching as desired.

8. Sew unit from step 6 between units from step 7 as shown. Press.

9. Sew unit from step 5 to unit from step 8. Press seam toward step 5 unit. Sew this unit between two 1" x 16½" Fabric A strips as shown. Press.

1   1

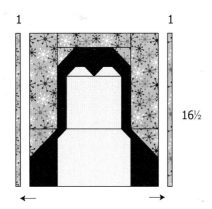

16½

Layering and Finishing

1. Referring to Layering the Quilt on page 126, arrange and baste backing, batting, and top together. Hand or machine quilt as desired.

2. To make scarf, fold one 4½" x 16" scarf strip in half lengthwise, right sides together. Sew using ¼"-wide seam along one short and one long side. Turn right side out, and press. Repeat for other piece. Determine desired length of scarf and cut strips to this measurement. Fold each strip's unfinished end under ¼" and press. Hand stitch strips folded edge to each side of penguin's neck. Loosely tie scarf, and tack in place if necessary.

3. Measure 1¼" from Holiday and bottom piece seam line on both sides of bottom piece and mark. Draw a line from this mark to center of bottom edge and back to mark as shown. Cut on marked line to make bottom angle edge. Trim batting and backing to ¼" beyond quilt top raw edges.

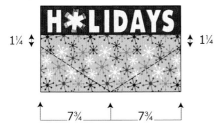

4. Fold one 3½" x 7½" binding piece in half lengthwise right sides together. Stitch a ¼"-wide seam on long side. Turn and press. Make three.

5. Fold tabs in half crosswise. Referring to photo for tab placement, place folded tabs on backing piece aligning raw edges and baste in place. Keep tabs in this position for next step.

6. Refer to Binding the Quilt on page 126. Use 2¾"-wide Binding strips to bind quilt. Note: Sew top and bottom angle edges first then sides. Leave an extra ¼" for turn-under on bottom side edges.

7. Fold tabs up and stitch in place along binding seam line.

I've grown pretty attached to penguins over the years especially after creating my Mummford Penguin character that made his way to fame with his guest role as "Hugsy" on the hit TV show, Friends. This particular penguin project was inspired by Chilly Weather from my 1998 book, Winter Follies. The updates to this guy are subtle but definitely freshen up his look. New modern colors along with a "nose job" and "chest reduction" brought this frosty fella into the 21st Century.

"Mummford"

1998
Chilly Weather
Originally featured in
Winter Follies

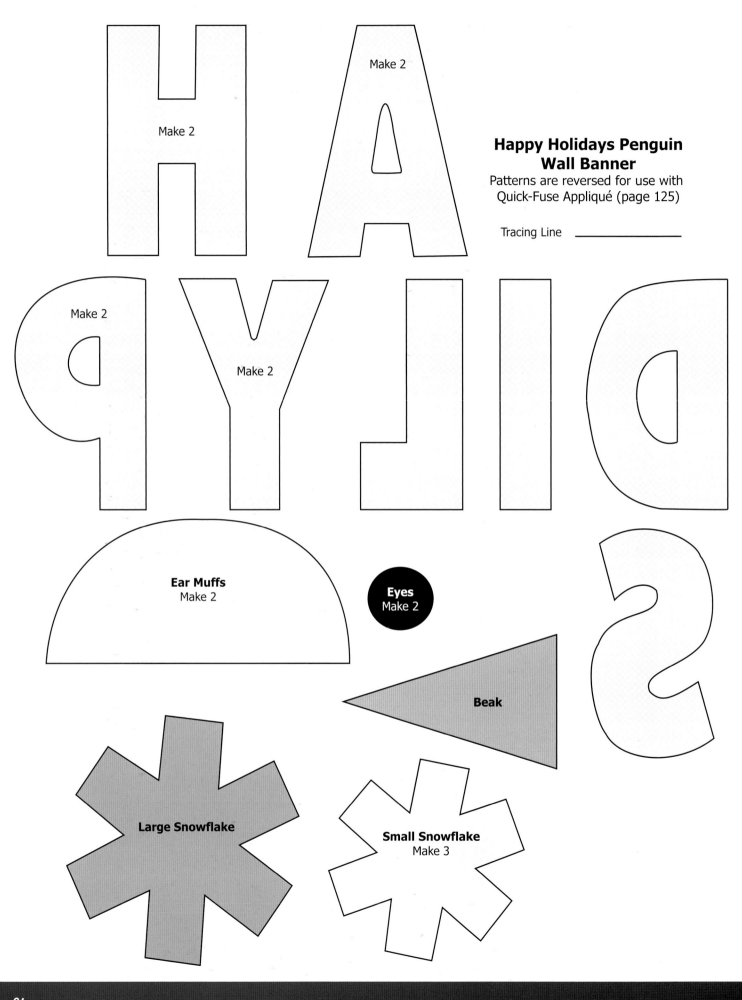

Make 2

Make 2

**Happy Holidays Penguin
Wall Banner**
Patterns are reversed for use with
Quick-Fuse Appliqué (page 125)

Tracing Line _____

Make 2

Make 2

Make 2

Ear Muffs
Make 2

Eyes
Make 2

Beak

Large Snowflake

Small Snowflake
Make 3

Frosty & Friends

wall ▪ quilt

Frosty & Friends Wall Quilt Finished Size: 27" x 35"	FIRST CUT		SECOND CUT	
	Number of Strips or Pieces	Dimensions	Number of Pieces	Dimensions
Fabric A Background ½ yard	2	2½" x 42"	4	2½" x 3½"
			24	2½" squares
	5	1½" x 42"	2	1½" x 27½"
			3	1½" x 17½"
			2	1½" x 12½"
			4	1½" x 2½"
			8	1½" x 2"
			12	1½" squares
Fabric B Snowman ½ yard	1	3½" x 42"	4	3½" x 4½"
	3	2½" x 42"	8	2½" x 7½"
			4	2½" x 4½"
	2	1½" x 42"	8	1½" x 4½"
			12	1½" squares
Fabric C Hat, Accent Border and Corners ⅓ yard	1	3½" x 42"	4	3½" squares
			4	2½" squares
	1	1½" x 42"	8	1½" x 1"
			8	1½" squares
	3	1" x 42"	2	1" x 28½"
			2	1" x 19½"
Fabric D Scarf ⅙ yard	2	1½" x 42"	4	1½" x 4½"
			4	1½" x 3½"
			4	1½" x 2½"
			4	1½" squares
Outside Border ⅙ yard* each of 7 Fabrics	2*	1½" x 42" *cut for each fabric		
Binding ⅜ yard	4	2¾" x 42"		

Appliqués - Assorted scraps
Backing - ⅞ yard
Batting - 31" x 39"
Embroidery Floss
Assorted Buttons - (8) ⅜" for eyes (24) ⅛" for mouths
Lightweight Fusible Web - ¼ yard

Fabric Requirements and Cutting Instructions

Read all instructions before beginning and use ¼"-wide seam allowances throughout. Read Cutting Strips and Pieces on page 124 prior to cutting fabric.

Getting Started

Let's have fun in the snow, inside that is, by making these cheery snowmen. Block measures 8½" x 12½" (unfinished). Refer to Accurate Seam Allowance on page 124. Whenever possible use Assembly Line Method on page 124. Press seams in direction of arrows.

Making the Block

1. Sew one 1½" x 2" Fabric A piece to one 1½" x 1" Fabric C piece as shown. Press. Make eight. Sew one 2½" Fabric C square between two of these units. Press. Make four.

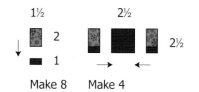

Make 8   Make 4

2. Sew one unit from step 1 between two 2½" Fabric A squares. Press. Make four.

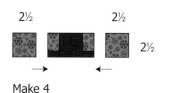

Make 4

3. Refer to Quick Corner Triangles on page 124. Making quick corner triangle units, sew two 1½" Fabric A squares to one 3½" x 4½" Fabric B piece as shown. Press. Make four.

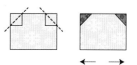

Fabric A = 1½ x 1½
Fabric B = 3½ x 4½
Make 4

1991
Frosty & Friends
Originally featured in
Quick Country Quilting

NOTES FROM *Debbie*

When I look at this quilt, I can't help but start to sing "Frosty, the Snowman." The expressions on the faces of these cheery guys always make me smile and make this quilt a contender for my favorite re-make. Of course, adding the faces was key to this update. As much as I love checkerboards, removing the red and ivory checkerboard and replacing it with a tonal tan check pattern made this design much cleaner. The snowy blizzard quilting in the border was stitched with silver metallic thread, adding just a touch of modern glitz.

---

4. Sew one 1½" x 2½" Fabric A piece to one 1½" Fabric D square as shown. Press. Make four. Sew one 1½" x 2½" Fabric D piece to one 1½" Fabric A square. Press. Make four.

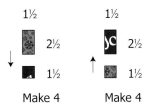

Make 4   Make 4

5. Arrange and sew together one 2½" x 3½" Fabric A piece, one unit from step 3, and two units from step 4, one of each combination as shown. Press. Make four.

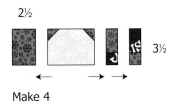

Make 4

6. Arrange and sew together two 1½" Fabric B squares and two 1½" Fabric C squares as shown. Press. Make four.

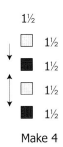

Make 4

7. Sew one 1½" x 3½" Fabric D piece to one 1½" Fabric B square as shown. Press. Make four. Arrange and sew together two 1½" x 4½" Fabric B pieces, one unit from step 6, and one unit from this step as shown. Press. Make four.

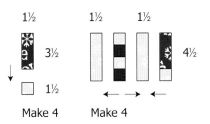

Make 4   Make 4

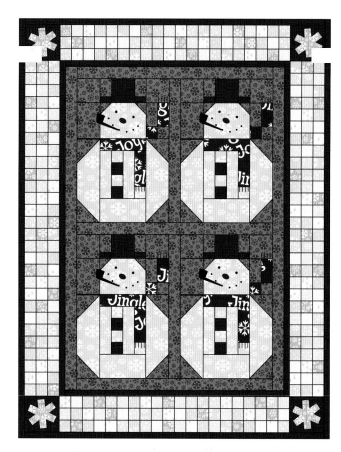

Frosty & Friends Wall Quilt
27" x 35"

10. Sew one unit from step 8 between two units from step 9 as shown. Press. Make four.

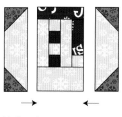

Make 4

11. Sew one unit from step 5 between one unit from step 2 and one unit from step 10 as shown. Press. Make four. Block measures 8½" x 12½".

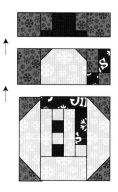

Make 4
Block measures 8½" x 12½"

8. Sew one unit from step 7 between one 1½" x 4½" Fabric D piece and one 2½" x 4½" Fabric B piece as shown. Press. Make four.

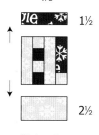

4½

1½

2½

Make 4

9. Making quick corner triangles, sew two 2½" Fabric A squares to one 2½" x 7½" Fabric B piece as shown. Press. Make eight.

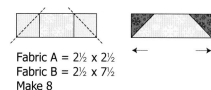

Fabric A = 2½ x 2½
Fabric B = 2½ x 7½
Make 8

Adding the Appliqués

Refer to appliqué instructions on page 125. Our instructions are for Quick-Fuse Appliqué, but if you prefer hand appliqué, reverse patterns and add ¼"-wide seam allowances.

1. Use patterns on page 101 to trace four snowflakes, pipe, and nose on paper side of fusible web. Use appropriate fabrics to prepare all appliqués for fusing.

2. Refer to photo on page 97 and layout to position and fuse appliqués to snowman blocks. Finish appliqué edges with machine satin stitch or other decorative stitching as desired.

3. Fuse snowflakes to 3½" Fabric C squares centering design and keeping appliqué away from seam allowance area. Finish snowflake edges with decorative stitches.

4. Refer to Embroidery Stitch Guide on page 127. Referring to photo on page 97, layout, and using a stem stitch, add fringe to both ends of scarves.

Assembling the Quilt

1. Referring to photo on page 97 and layout on page 100, sew one 1½" x 12½" Fabric A piece between two snowman blocks. Press seams toward Fabric A. Make two.

2. Referring to photo on page 97 and layout on page 100, sew three 1½" x 17½" Fabric A strips and rows from step 1 together. Press seams toward Fabric A. Sew this unit between two 1½" x 27½" Fabric A strips. Press.

3. Sew two 1" x 19½" Fabric C strips to top and bottom of quilt. Press seams toward Fabric C. Sew two 1" x 28½" Fabric C strips to sides of quilt. Press.

4. Sew together lengthwise seven 1½" x 42" Outside Border strips, one of each fabric as shown to make a strip set. Press seams in one direction. Make two, one as shown and one with fabrics in a different combination. Cut strip set into forty-eight 1½"-wide segments as shown.

1½

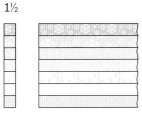

Make 2
Cut 48 segments

5. Sew four strips from step 4 together end-to-end to make one 1½" x 28½" strip. Make twelve.

6. Referring to photo on page 97 and layout on page 100, sew three strips from step 5 together making sure same fabrics don't touch each other. Press. Make two. Sew these units to sides of quilt. Press seams toward Fabric C.

7. Top and bottom rows consist of three rows each. Remaining strips are longer than needed. Stagger rows so same fabrics don't touch each other. Determine the beginning and ending of each row and remove extra pieces. Strips need to measure 1½" x 20½". Sew three of these rows together. Press. Make two.

8. Sew one unit from step 7 between two 3½" Fabric C squares. Press seams toward Fabric C. Make two. Sew to top and bottom of quilt. Press.

9. Referring to photo on page 97 and layout on page 100, sew buttons to each block for snowman's eyes and mouth. Note: Buttons can be sewn to snowmen after quilting is completed if desired.

Layering and Finishing

1. Referring to Layering the Quilt on page 126, arrange and baste backing, batting, and top together. Hand or machine quilt as desired.

2. Refer to Binding the Quilt on page 126. Use 2¾"-wide binding strips to bind quilt.

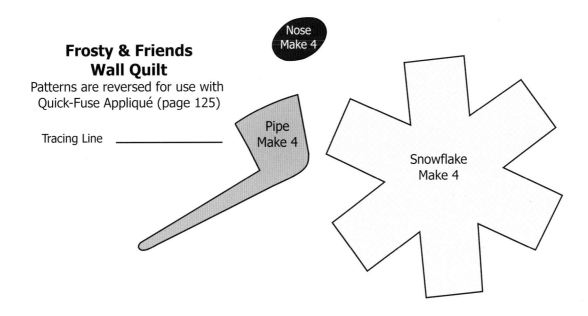

Frosty & Friends Wall Quilt
Patterns are reversed for use with Quick-Fuse Appliqué (page 125)

Tracing Line _____

Nose
Make 4

Pipe
Make 4

Snowflake
Make 4

Greeter Santa

door ▪ banner

Greeter Santa Door Banner Finished Size: 24" x 51"	FIRST CUT		SECOND CUT	
	Number of Strips or Pieces	Dimensions	Number of Pieces	Dimensions
Fabric A Background ½ yard	1	5" x 42"	1	5" x 6½"
			4	3½" squares
			1	3" x 3½"
			1	2½" x 6½"
			2	2½" x 3½"
	5	1½" x 42"	2	1½" x 16½"
			2	1½" x 12"
			2	1½" x 3½"
			2	1½" x 2"
			4	1½" squares
Fabric B Santa Coat ⅝ yard	2	4½" x 42"	2	4½" x 23½"
	1	3½" x 42"	2	3½" x 13½"
			1	3½" x 10"
	1	2½" x 42"	2	2½" x 12"
	1	2" x 42"	2	2" x 6½"
			2	2" squares
			3	1½" squares
Fabric C Santa Coat Trim ¼ yard	1	3½" x 42"	1	3½" x 16½"
			1	2½" x 23½"
	1	2" x 42"	2	2" x 3½"
			1	1½" x 7½"
Fabric D Face Scrap	1	2½" x 4½"		
Fabric E Hair & Beard Obese Eighth	1	7½" square		
	2	2" x 2½"		
Fabric F Mitten & Boots ⅙ yard	1	3½" x 42"	2	3½" squares
			2	2½" x 8½"
			2	2½" x 5½"
			2	1½" squares
First Border ⅙ yard	4	1" x 42"	2	1" x 18½"
Outside Border ⅓ yard	4	2½" x 42"	2	2½" x 19½"
Binding ½ yard	5	2¾" x 42"		

Appliqués* - Assorted scraps
Backing - 1⅝ yards
Batting - 28" x 55"
Lightweight Fusible Web - Scraps
⅜" Buttons - 2 for eyes
Optional: Bell & Ribbon Embellishments
*We used Berber for the coat and boot trims.

Fabric Requirements and Cutting Instructions

Read all instructions before beginning and use ¼"-wide seam allowances throughout. Read Cutting Strips and Pieces on page 124 prior to cutting fabric.

Getting Started

This jolly fellow will welcome family and friends to your festive holiday gatherings. This quilt is constructed in three sections: top (head), middle (body), and bottom (feet). Refer to Accurate Seam Allowance on page 124. Whenever possible use Assembly Line Method on page 124. Press seams in direction of arrows.

Making the Quilt

Pay close attention to diagrams and fabric orientation prior to sewing the pieces together.

1. Refer to Quick Corner Triangles on page 124. Making quick corner triangle units, sew two 3½" Fabric A squares to one 3½" x 10" Fabric B piece as shown. Press.

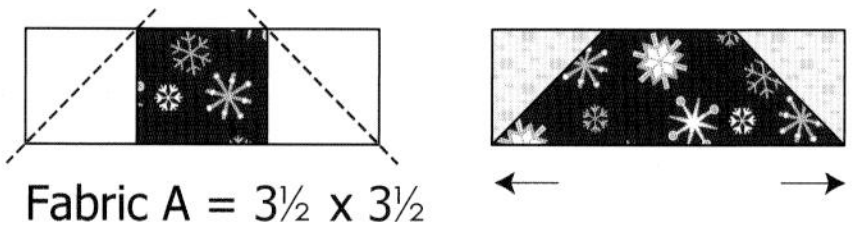

Fabric A = 3½ x 3½
Fabric B = 3½ x 10

2. Making a quick corner triangle unit, sew one 1½" Fabric B square to one 3" x 3½" Fabric A piece as shown. Press.

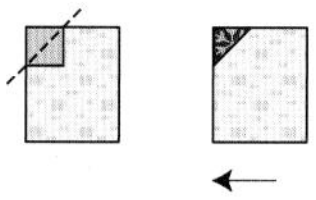

Fabric B = 1½ x 1½
Fabric A = 3 x 3½

3. Sew one 2½" x 4½" Fabric D piece between two 2" x 2½" Fabric E pieces as shown. Press. Sew one 1½" x 7½" Fabric C piece to unit. Press. Sew unit from step 2 to unit from this step as shown. Press.

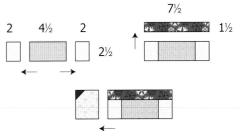

4. Sew unit from step 1 to unit from step 3 as shown. Press. Sew this unit between one 2½" x 6½" Fabric A piece and one 5" x 6½" Fabric A piece as shown. Press. Sew one 1½" x 16½" Fabric A strip to top of unit. Press. This completes the top section.

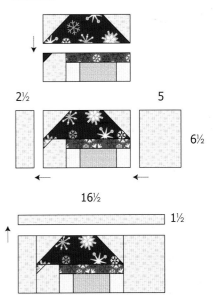

5. Making quick corner triangle units, sew two 2" Fabric B squares to one 7½" Fabric E square as shown. Press.

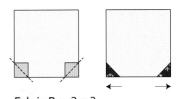

Fabric B = 2 x 2
Fabric E = 7½ x 7½

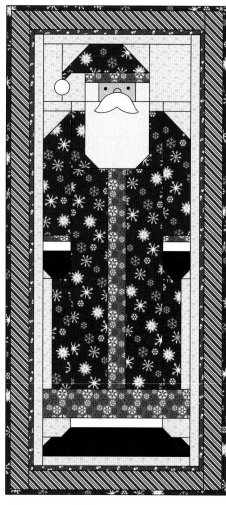

Greeter Santa Door Banner
24" x 51"

6. Sew one 1½" x 2" Fabric A piece to one 2" x 6½" Fabric B piece as shown. Press. Make two. Sew unit from step 5 between units from this step as shown. Press.

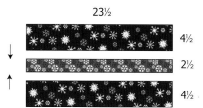

Make 2

7. Sew one 2½" x 23½" Fabric C strip between two 4½" x 23½" Fabric B strips as shown. Press. Refer to layout to sew unit from step 6 to top of unit from this step. Press seams toward bottom unit.

23½

4½

2½

4½

8. Making a quick corner triangle unit, sew one 3½" Fabric A square to one 3½" x 13½" Fabric B strip as shown. Press. Sew one 1½" x 3½" Fabric A piece to unit. Press. Make two, one of each variation.

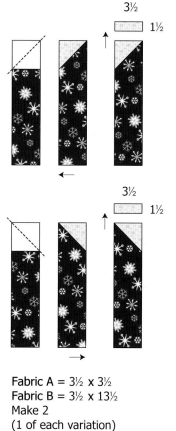

Fabric A = 3½ x 3½
Fabric B = 3½ x 13½
Make 2
(1 of each variation)

Tracing Line _____

Placement Line -·-·-·-·-·-·-·-

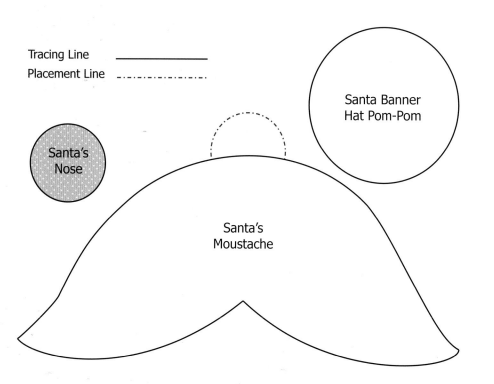

Santa's Nose

Santa Banner Hat Pom-Pom

Santa's Moustache

9. Making quick corner triangle units, sew one 1½" Fabric A square and one 1½" Fabric B square to one 3½" Fabric F square as shown. Press. Sew one 2" x 3½" Fabric C piece to unit from this step. Press. Make two, one of each variation.

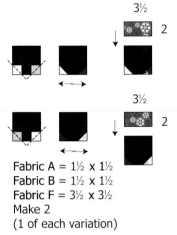

Fabric A = 1½ x 1½
Fabric B = 1½ x 1½
Fabric F = 3½ x 3½
Make 2
(1 of each variation)

10. Sew one 1½" x 12" Fabric A piece to one 2½" x 12" Fabric B piece. Press seams toward Fabric B. Make two. Sew one unit from step 9 between unit from step 8 and unit from this step. Press. Make two, one of each variation. Sew unit from step 7 between units from this step. Press. This completes the middle section.

The Magic of Santa (circa 1994) was my first self-published small book and the Santa Door Banner has been our most requested design. So, I just had to include this project in my 25th anniversary review. I updated the colors – basically making everything brighter – but I kept the traditional quality of a folk art Santa. Small alterations like adding boots, Berber trims, and silver bells freshen the design and a more expressive face makes him a cheerier guy – he is Santa, after all!

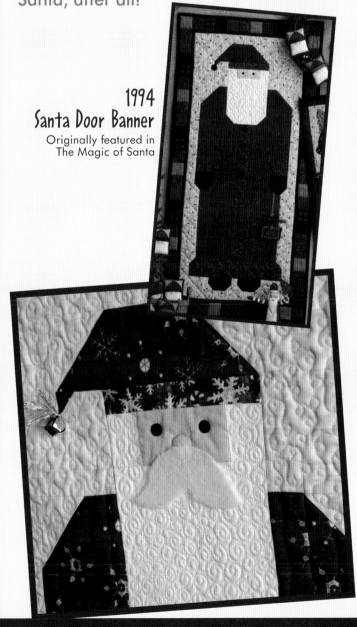

1994
Santa Door Banner
Originally featured in
The Magic of Santa

11. Making a quick corner triangle unit, sew one 1½"
Fabric F square to one 2½" x 3½" Fabric A piece
as shown. Sew this unit to one 2½" x 5½" Fabric
F piece as shown. Press. Make two, one of each
variation. Referring to step 13 diagram, sew units
together. Press.

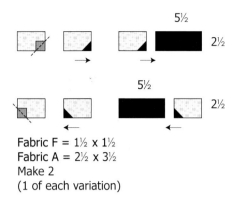

Fabric F = 1½ x 1½
Fabric A = 2½ x 3½
Make 2
(1 of each variation)

12. Making a quick corner triangle unit, sew one 1½"
Fabric A square to one 2½" x 8½" Fabric F piece
as shown. Press. Make two, one of each variation.
Referring to step 13 diagram, sew units together.
Press.

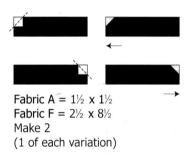

Fabric A = 1½ x 1½
Fabric F = 2½ x 8½
Make 2
(1 of each variation)

13. Arrange and sew together, one 3½" x 16½" Fabric
C piece, unit from step 11, unit from step 12, and
one 1½" x 16½" Fabric A strip as shown. Press. This
completes the bottom section.

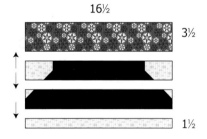

14. Referring to photo on page 103 and layout on page
104, arrange and sew together top, middle and
bottom sections. Press.

15. Sew three 1½" x 42" Fabric A strips together end-to-
end to make one continuous strip. Cut two
1½" x 45½" strips and sew to sides of unit from step
14. Press.

Adding the Borders

1. Refer to Adding the Borders on page 125. Sew two
1" x 18½" First Border strips to top and bottom of
quilt. Press seams toward border. Sew remaining
1" x 42" First Border strips together end-to-end to
make one continuous 1"-wide First Border strip.
Measure quilt through center from top to bottom
including borders just added. Cut two 1"-wide First
Border strips to this measurement. Sew to sides of
quilt. Press.

2. Sew 2½" x 19½" Outside Border strips to top and
bottom of quilt. Press seams toward border just
sewn. Refer to step 1 to join, measure, trim, and
sew 2½"-wide Outside Border strips to sides of quilt.
Press.

Adding the Appliqués
Refer to appliqué
instructions on page 125. Our instructions are for Quick-
Fuse Appliqué, but if you prefer hand appliqué, reverse
patterns and add ¼"-wide seam allowances.

1. Use patterns on page 104 to trace hat pom-pom,
Santa's nose, and moustache on paper side of
fusible web. For fur trim on sleeves and boots, draw
on paper side of fusible web two 1" x 3" rectangles
for cuff sections and one 1" x 10" rectangle for
boot section. Use appropriate fabrics to prepare all
appliqués for fusing. Optional: Refer to photo on
page 103 for ideas. If desired, use bells and ribbons
for hat embellishment and add more bells and
ribbon to one hand. We lightly stuffed Santa's nose.
We elected to wait and appliqué the Berber pieces to
the quilt after quilting was completed.

2. Refer to photo on page 103 and layout on page
104 to position and fuse appliqués to quilt. Finish
appliqué edges with machine straight stitch, satin
stitch or other decorative stitching as desired.

Layering and Finishing

1. Referring to Layering the Quilt on page 126, arrange
and baste backing, batting, and top together. Hand
or machine quilt as desired.

2. Refer to Binding the Quilt on page 126. Use 2¾"-
wide binding strips to bind quilt.

Santa Pockets

card ∎ holder

Santa Pockets Card Holder Finished Size: 15½" x 32¾"	FIRST CUT		SECOND CUT	
	Number of Strips or Pieces	Dimensions	Number of Pieces	Dimensions
Fabric A Block Background ⅛ yard each of 3 Fabrics	1*	2" x 42" *cut for each fabric	1* 4* 3* 2*	2" x 2½" 2" x 1½" 1½" squares 1" x 1¾"
Fabric B Santa's Hat & Suit ⅛ yard each of 3 Fabrics	1*	2½" x 42" *cut for each fabric	1* 2* 3*	2½" x 3½" 2" x 3" 1½" squares
Fabric C Hair & Beard Scraps each of 3 Fabrics	1* 2*	3½" x 3" 1" x 1½" *cut for each fabric		
Fabric D Face Scraps	3	1½" x 2½"		
Fabric E Hat Brim Scraps each of 3 Fabrics	1*	1" x 4" *cut for each fabric		
Fabric F Quilt Background & Block Accent ⅝ yard	1 1 1	11" x 42" 7½" x 42" 1" x 42"	1 3 3 3 6	11" x 28¼" 7½" x 7¾" 7½" x 1¼" 7½" x 1" 1" x 6½"
Accent Border ⅛ yard	2	1" x 42"	2 2	1" x 28¼" 1" x 11"
Outside Border ⅓ yard	3	2½" x 42"	2 2	2½" x 32¼" 2½" x 11"
Binding ⅓ yard	3	2¾" x 42"		

Appliqués - Scraps
Backing - ⅝ yard
Batting - 20" x 37"
Heavyweight Fusible Web - ⅛ yard
⅛" Buttons - 6 for eyes
1" Buttons - 3 for pom-pom
Note: Yardage is for non-directional fabric. If using directional fabric, adjust yardage and fabric direction accordingly.

Fabric Requirements and Cutting Instructions
Read all instructions before beginning and use ¼"-wide seam allowances throughout. Read Cutting Strips and Pieces on page 124 prior to cutting fabric.

Getting Started
Display your holiday cards by making this jolly quilt. This cardholder is constructed and quilted prior to sewing on the decorative Santa pockets. Refer to Accurate Seam Allowance on page 124. Whenever possible use Assembly Line Method on page 124. Press seams in direction of arrows.

Making the Quilt

1. Fold two 1" x 11" Accent Border pieces in half lengthwise wrong sides together to make two ½" x 11" folded pieces. Press. Repeat step using two 1" x 28¼" Accent strips to make two ½" x 28¼" folded pieces.

2. Matching raw edges, layer two folded 11" strips from step 1 to top and bottom of 11" x 28¼" Fabric F piece. Baste in place. Baste 28¼" folded strips to sides of unit.

3. Sew two 2½" x 11" Outside Border strips to top and bottom of unit from step 2. Press seams toward border. Sew two 2½" x 32¼" Outside Border strips to sides of unit. Press.

Layering and Finishing
Quilting and Binding are completed prior to attaching Santa pockets to quilt.

1. Referring to Layering the Quilt on page 126, arrange and baste backing, batting, and top together. Hand or machine quilt as desired.

2. Refer to Binding the Quilt on page 126. Use 2¾"-wide binding strips to bind quilt.

1993
Sew Many Santas
Originally featured in
Quick Country
Christmas Quilts

Back in 1993 when I first created this project for Quick Country Christmas Quilts, the trend was to use colors and fabrics that were dark and had an aged and antique look. In fact, these colors were signature to most of my art and designs during that era. I remember "tea-dying" fabrics to make them look even more aged. Today, colors are cleaner and brighter. I became an instant fan of bright lime green early in the trend and painted my entire family room and kitchen in that color. Brown has become a favorite neutral and adding that and my favorite green to a Christmas project is fun and unexpected. Notice the Berber trim added to the pockets!

Making the Santa Pockets

This quilt has three Santa pockets using different fabric combinations. When sewing units and pieces together match all fabrics within each block.

1. Refer to Quick Corner Triangles on page 124. Making a quick corner triangle unit, sew one 1½" Fabric A square to one 2½" x 3½" Fabric B piece as shown. Press. Make three, one of each combination.

Fabric A = 1½ x 1½
Fabric B = 2½ x 3½
Make 3
(1 of each combination)

2. Making a quick corner triangle, sew one 1½" Fabric B square to one 2" x 1½" Fabric A piece as shown. Press. Sew this unit to one 2" x 1½" Fabric A piece. Press. Make three, one of each combination.

2

1½

Fabric B = 1½ x 1½
Fabric A = 2 x 1½
Make 3
(1 of each combination)

3. Sew one unit from step 1 between one 2" x 2½" Fabric A piece and one unit from step 2. Press. Make three, one of each combination.

2

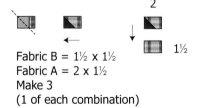

2½

Make 3
(1 of each combination)

4. Sew one 1" x 4" Fabric E piece between two 1" x 1¾" Fabric A pieces as shown. Press. Make three, one of each combination.

1¾   4   1¾

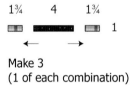   1

Make 3
(1 of each combination)

5. Arrange and sew together two 2" x 1½" Fabric A pieces, two 1" x 1½" Fabric C pieces, and one 1½" x 2½" Fabric D piece as shown. Press. Make three, one of each combination.

2   1   2½   1   2

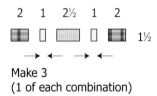   1½

Make 3
(1 of each combination)

6. Making a quick corner triangle unit, sew one 1½" Fabric A square to one 2" x 3" Fabric B piece as shown. Press. Make three, one of each combination.

Fabric A = 1½ x 1½
Fabric B = 2 x 3
Make 3
(1 of each combination)

7. Making a quick corner triangle unit, sew one 1½" Fabric A square to one 2" x 3" Fabric B piece as shown. Press. Make three, one of each combination.

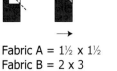

Fabric A = 1½ x 1½
Fabric B = 2 x 3
Make 3
(1 of each combination)

8. Making quick corner triangle units, sew two 1½" Fabric B squares to one 3½" x 3" Fabric C piece as shown. Press. Make three, one of each combination.

Fabric B = 1½ x 1½
Fabric C = 3½ x 3
Make 3
(1 of each combination)

9. Sew one unit from step 8 between one unit from step 6 and one unit from step 7 as shown. Press. Make three, one of each combination.

Make 3
(1 of each combination)

10. Arrange and sew together matching units from steps 3, 4, 5, and 9 as shown. Press. Make three, one of each combination.

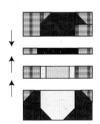

Make 3
(1 of each combination)

Santa Pockets Card Holder
Mustache

Make 3

Optional
Pom-Pom
Make 3

11. Sew two 1" x 6½" Fabric F pieces to sides of unit from step 10. Sew this unit between one 7½" x 1¼" Fabric F piece and one 7½" x 1" Fabric F piece as shown. Press. Make three, one of each combination.

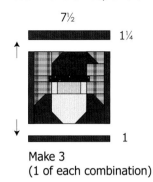

7½
1¼
1

Make 3
(1 of each combination)

12. Referring to Layering the Quilt on page 126, layer and center pocket and 7½" x 7¾" Fabric F backing piece right sides together on batting, wrong side of backing on batting. Using ¼"-wide seam, stitch around all edges, leaving a 4" opening on one side for turning. Trim batting close to stitching and backing even with pocket edges. Clip corners, turn, and press. Hand-stitch opening closed.

13. Machine or hand quilt as desired.

Adding the Appliqués

Refer to appliqué instructions on page 125. Our instructions are for Quick-Fuse Appliqué, but if you prefer hand appliqué, add ¼"-wide seam allowances.

1. Use pattern to trace three mustaches and three ¾" x 6" rectangles on paper side of fusible web. Use appropriate fabrics to prepare all appliqués for fusing. Note: We used Berber for pocket trim and moustache.

2. Refer to photo on page 107 to position and fuse appliqués to each pocket (¾" x 6" piece is fused to top edge of pocket. Trim length if necessary). Note: Heavyweight fusible web was used for appliqués, making it possible to leave edges free of stitching. If quilt is to be cleaned, use lightweight fusible web instead and finish all appliqué edges with machine satin stitch or other decorative stitching as desired.

3. Sew buttons for hat pom-pom and Santa's eyes to each block.

4. Referring to photo on page 107, arrange each pocket on quilt leaving 1¼" between each pocket and placing them 1¼" from top and bottom edges.

5. Referring to Embroidery Stitches on page 127 and using a blind stitch or machine blind hem stitch, sew pockets to quilt along bottom and side edges.

Sunflower Power

dimensional wall ■ quilt

Sunflower Power Dimensional Wall Quilt Finished Size: 34" x 28"	FIRST CUT		SECOND CUT	
	Number of Strips or Pieces	Dimensions	Number of Pieces	Dimensions
Fabric A Center ⅓ yard	2	4½" x 42"	9	4½" x 6½"
Fabric B Block 1st Border ⅜ yard	7	1½" x 42"	18 18	1½" x 8½" 1½" x 4½"
Fabric C Block 2nd Border - Light ⅙ yard	4	1" x 42"	9 9	1" x 9" 1" x 6½"
Fabric D Block 2nd Border - Dark ⅙ yard	4	1" x 42"	9 9	1" x 9½" 1" x 7"
Fabric E Block 3rd Border - Light ¼ yard	5	1" x 42"	9 9	1" x 10" 1" x 7½"
Fabric F Block 3rd Border - Dark ¼ yard	5	1" x 42"	9 9	1" x 10½" 1" x 8"
First Border ⅙ yard	4	1" x 42"	2 2	1" x 30½" 1" x 25½"
Outside Border ¼ yard	4	1½" x 42"	2 2	1½" x 31½" 1½" x 27½"
Binding ⅜ yard	4	2¾" x 42"		

Appliqué Flower Centers - ⅙ yard
Appliqué Petals & Leaves - Assorted scraps
Backing - 1 yard
Batting - 38" x 32"
Lighweight Fusible Web - 1 yard
Template Plastic or Pattern Paper

Fabric Requirements and Cutting Instructions
Read all instructions before beginning and use ¼"-wide seam allowances throughout. Read Cutting Strips and Pieces on page 124 prior to cutting fabric.

Getting Started
Sunflowers pop from this sensational quilt due to a combination of dimensional petals and quick-fused appliqués. Block measures 10½" x 8½" (unfinished). Refer to Accurate Seam Allowance on page 124. Whenever possible use Assembly Line Method on page 124. Press seams in direction of arrows.

Making the Block

1. Sew one 4½" x 6½" Fabric A piece between two 1½" x 4½" Fabric B pieces as shown. Press. Make nine.

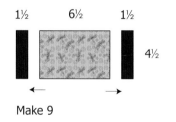

Make 9

2. Sew one unit from step 1 between two 1½" x 8½" Fabric B pieces as shown. Press. Make nine.

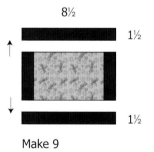

Make 9

3. Sew one 1" x 6½" Fabric C piece to one unit from step 2 as shown. Press. Sew one 1" x 9" Fabric C piece to top of unit. Press. Make nine.

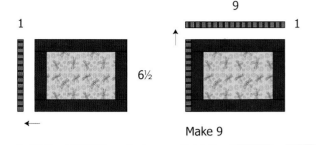

Make 9

4. Sew one 1" x 7" Fabric D piece to one unit from step 3 as shown. Press. Sew one 1" x 9½" Fabric D piece to bottom of unit. Press. Make nine.

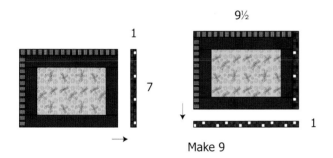

Make 9

5. Sew one 1" x 7½" Fabric E piece to one unit from step 4 as shown. Press. Sew one 1" x 10" Fabric E piece to top of unit. Press. Make nine.

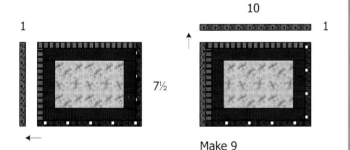

Make 9

Sunflowers have the power to make us feel the warmth of sunshine and bring back summer nostalgia all in a single glance. That is why I love them and have interpreted them in my quilts and art many times. For this project I referenced the pieced log cabin background in Fruit Orchard from Greenwood Gardens (2007) and the dimensional sunflowers from the wall art piece called Sunshine Tea from the 2003 book, Best Loved Quilting Themes. Since this wall quilt has nine sunflowers I realized that it was going to add up to making almost 100 dimensional petals. Yikes! By only making a few dimensional petals in each flower and then appliquéing the rest, we saved a lot of time and still maintained the dimensional quality.

2003
Sunshine Tea
Originally featured in
Best Loved
Quilting Themes

2007
Fruit Orchard
Originally featured in
Greenwood Gardens

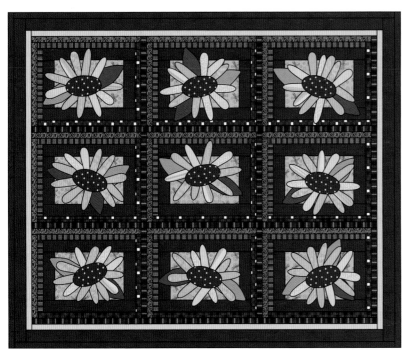

Sunflower Power Dimensional Wall Quilt
34" x 28"

6. Sew one 1" x 8" Fabric F piece to one unit from step 5 as shown. Press. Sew one 1" x 10½" Fabric F piece to bottom of unit. Press. Make nine. Block measures 10½" x 8½".

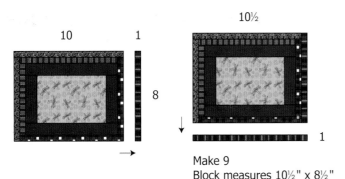

Make 9
Block measures 10½" x 8½"

Adding the Appliqués

Quilt shown uses seven different fabrics for petals and two different fabrics for leaves. Refer to appliqué instructions on page 125. Our instructions use a combination of Quick-Fuse and Dimensional Appliqué. If you prefer hand appliqué, reverse patterns and add ¼"-wide seam allowances. The number of leaves and flower petals vary from block to block. Each block has two or three leaves, three to four dimensional flower petals, and six to nine fused flower petals. Extra flower petals and leaves are made to allow for placement options when laying out blocks. Refer to photo on page 111 and layout to arrange appliqués on each block.

1. Trace and cut a template using Flower Center and Dimensional Flower Petal patterns on page 115.

2. Cut eighteen 2½" x 4" pieces from flower center fabric. Using flower center template, trace pattern on wrong side of nine pieces of fabric. Layer one marked fabric and one unmarked fabric right sides together on batting scrap, wrong side of unmarked piece on batting.

3. Sew on traced line. Trim flower center batting close to stitching and seams to ³⁄₁₆". Clip curves. Make a slit in the center of marked piece being careful not to cut the other fabric. Turn right side out and press. Make nine.

4. Using dimensional flower petal pattern, trace petals on the wrong side of fabric. Leave ½" space between each petal when tracing several petals from one fabric piece. Layer marked fabric on matching backing fabric right sides together. Stitch on traced curved lines leaving end open for turning. Trim fabric ³⁄₁₆" from stitching line, clip curves, and turn right side out and press. Make thirty to thirty-six petals from assorted fabrics.

5. To create a dimensional look, gently pinch open end of petal and stitch to hold fold in place.

6. Use patterns on page 115 to trace flower petals and leaves on paper side of fusible web. Use appropriate fabrics to prepare all appliqués for fusing.

7. Refer to photo on page 111 and layout to position leaves, petals, and center on block. Carefully remove dimensional petals and center. Fuse other pieces in place. Finish appliqué edges with machine satin stitch or other decorative stitching as desired.

8. Reposition dimensional petals and flower center on block, making sure petals extend under flower center. Hand or machine stitch flower center to block. This will hold dimensional petals in place. Make nine.

Assembling and Finishing the Quilt

1. Referring to photo on page 111 and layout on page 114. Arrange and sew together, three rows with three blocks each. Press seams in opposite direction from row to row.

2. Sew rows together. Press.

3. Refer to Adding the Borders on page 126. Sew two 1" x 30½" First Border strips to top and bottom of quilt. Press seams toward border. Sew two 1" x 25½" First Border strips to sides of quilt. Press.

4. Sew two 1½" x 31½" Outside Border strips to top and bottom of quilt. Press seams toward border. Sew two 1½" x 27½" Outside Border strips to sides of quilt. Press.

5. Referring to Layering the Quilt on page 126, arrange and baste backing, batting, and top together. Hand or machine quilt as desired.

6. Refer to Binding the Quilt on page 126. Use 2¾"-wide binding strips to bind quilt.

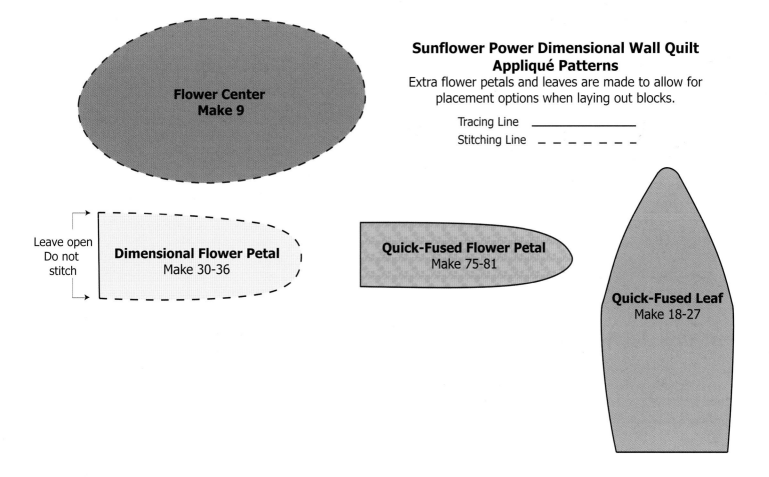

Flower Center
Make 9

Dimensional Flower Petal
Make 30-36

Leave open
Do not
stitch

Sunflower Power Dimensional Wall Quilt Appliqué Patterns

Extra flower petals and leaves are made to allow for placement options when laying out blocks.

Tracing Line ──────────

Stitching Line ─ ─ ─ ─ ─ ─

Quick-Fused Flower Petal
Make 75-81

Quick-Fused Leaf
Make 18-27

French Linen Kitchen
wall ■ art

French Linen Kitchen Wall Art Finished Size: 17½" x 23"	FIRST CUT	
	Number of Strips or Pieces	Dimensions
Fabric A Background Kitchen Towel or ⅝ yard	1	17½" x 19½"
Fabric B Tabletop ⅛ yard	1	1½" x 17½"
Fabric C Table & Bottom Binding ⅙ yard	1 1	3½" x 17½" 2¼" x 20"
Binding Top & Sides Kitchen Towel or ¼ yard	1 2 2	2¼" x width of towel 2¼" x length of towel or 2¼" x 42"
Bowl Rim & Base - Napkin or assorted scraps Bowl - Napkin or scrap Pear Appliqués - Assorted scraps Backing - ⅔ yard Batting - 22" x 27" Lightweight Fusible Web - ¾ yard		

Fabric Requirements and Cutting Instructions
Read all instructions before beginning and use ¼"-wide seam allowances throughout.

Getting Started
This quilt uses two-kitchen towels and two different napkins to create the dimensional wallhanging. Yardage has been provided in chart if fabric is desired for this project.

Making the Quilt
Refer to appliqué instructions on page 125. Our instructions are for Quick-Fuse Appliqué, but if you prefer hand appliqué, reverse patterns and add ¼"-wide seam allowances.

1. Referring to photo, sew one 1½" x 17½" Fabric B strip between one 17½" x 19½" Fabric A piece and one 3½" x 17½" Fabric C strip as shown. Press.

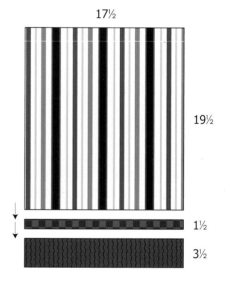

2. Use patterns on page 118 to trace pears, stems, leaves and bowl on paper side of fusible web. Use appropriate fabrics to prepare all appliqués for fusing. Do not trace the bowl rim at this time. Note: Refer to photo for quantity of leaves needed for this project. We have two units with two leaves each and three units with one leaf each.

3. Refer to photo to position and fuse appliqués to quilt. Finish appliqué edges with machine satin stitch or other decorative stitching as desired.

4. Trace bowl rim on pattern paper and cut on traced line. Trace pattern on wrong side of rim fabric. Traced line will be sewing line.

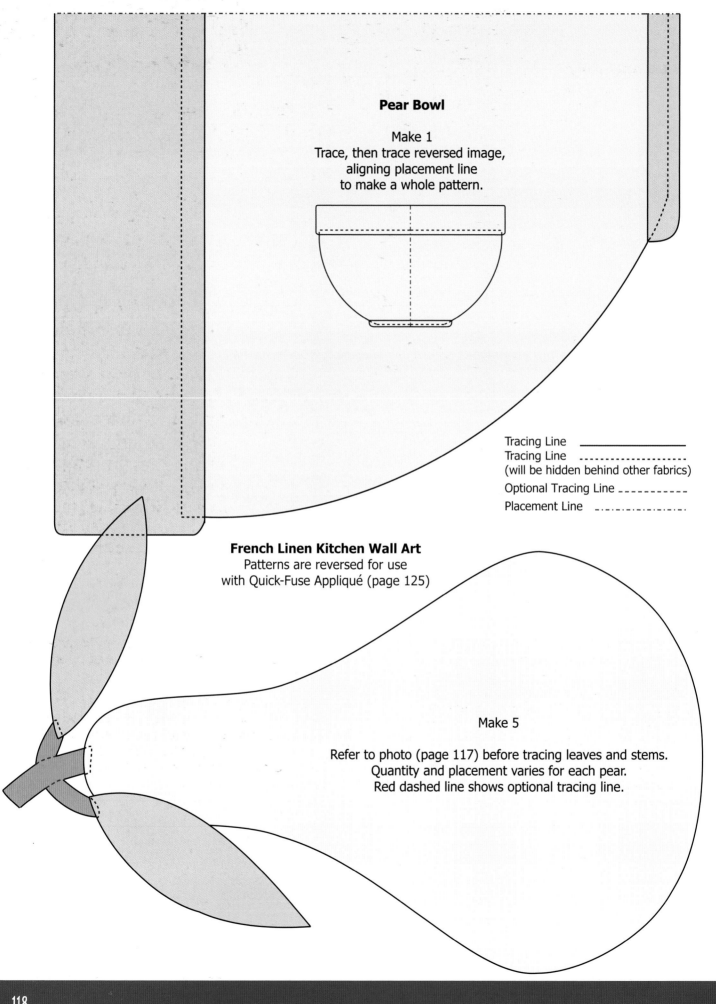

Pear Bowl

Make 1
Trace, then trace reversed image,
aligning placement line
to make a whole pattern.

Tracing Line ————————
Tracing Line ....
(will be hidden behind other fabrics)
Optional Tracing Line – – – – – –
Placement Line –..–..–..–..–

French Linen Kitchen Wall Art
Patterns are reversed for use
with Quick-Fuse Appliqué (page 125)

Make 5

Refer to photo (page 117) before tracing leaves and stems.
Quantity and placement varies for each pear.
Red dashed line shows optional tracing line.

2003
Pear Perfection
Originally featured in
Quilts from a
Gardener's Journal

Pear Perfection was showcased in our award-winning 2003 book, Quilts from a Gardener's Journal. This book was really fun to create as we used a couple different gardens nurtured by staff members as photo locations. This small grapevine arbor in Jackie's backyard was a fabulous spot to do our photography for this unique project. To update this one, I really, really, simplified the design and came up with the idea of using kitchen linens as the main fabrics which make it even more suitable for a kitchen setting. The background stripe is a kitchen towel and the bowl and bowl rim are made from napkins. To keep things easy, the iron scroll is simply hanging on the wall directly above the project.

5. Layer traced bowl rim piece and backing right sides together on batting, wrong side of backing on batting. Stitch on traced line. Trim batting close to stitching. Trim rim and backing scant ¼" from stitching line. Make a slit through the batting and backing piece being careful not to cut the rim fabric. Turn right side out and press. Add quilting if desired.

6. Referring to photo on page 117, place rim on bowl. Hand appliqué rim to quilt using a blind stitch (page 127).

7. Referring to Layering the Quilt on page 126, arrange and baste backing, batting, and top together. Hand or machine quilt as desired.

8. Refer to Binding the Quilt on page 126. Use 2¼"-wide binding strips to bind quilt. Note: Binding was made from kitchen towel and sewn to top and sides of quilt. Fabric C binding piece was sewn to bottom edge of quilt. Finished width of binding is ¼" instead of our normal ½".

Button Collection
shadow ▪ box

Button Collection Shadow Box Finished Size: 12" square (inside measurement)	FIRST CUT		SECOND CUT	
	Number of Strips or Pieces	Dimensions	Number of Pieces	Dimensions
Fabric A Background ⅜ yard	1	4½" x 42"	1	4½" x 5"
			1	3¼" x 4½"
			1	3½" x 2"
			2	1" x 1½"
			2	1" x 1¼"
			8	1" squares
	2	2½" x 42"	2	2½" x 15½"
			2	2½" x 12"
Fabric B Jars Fat Eighth	1	5" square		
	1	4½" x 6"		
	1	3½" x 7"		
Fabric C Lids Assorted scraps	1	1¼" x 3½"		
	1	1½" x 2½"		
	1	1" x 4"		
Fabric D Shelf Background ¼ yard	1	3½" x 42"	2	3½" x 18½"
	1	2½" x 42"	1	2½" x 12"
Fabric E Shelf Light Accent ⅛ yard	1	1¼" x 42"	1	1¼" x 18½"
Fabric F Shelf Dark Accent ⅛ yard	1	1" x 42"	1	1" x 18½"

Hinged Shadow Box with 12" opening
⅛ " Foam Core Board
Assorted Decorative Buttons
Glue & Tape
Sawtooth Picture Hanger (optional)

Note: Fabrics D, E & F are cut to fit 12" Shadow Box. If using a different size frame adjust cut sizes.

Fabric Requirements and Cutting Instructions
Read all instructions before beginning and use ¼"-wide seam allowances throughout. Read Cutting Strips and Pieces on page 124 prior to cutting fabric.

Getting Started
Here's a great way to showcase that special collection of decorative buttons. Refer to Accurate Seam Allowance on page 124. Press seams in direction of arrows.

Making the Wall Art

1. Refer to Quick Corner Triangles on page 124. Making quick corner triangle units, sew two 1" Fabric A squares to one 4½" x 6" Fabric B piece as shown to make Unit 1. Press. Repeat step to sew two 1" Fabric A squares to 3½" x 7" Fabric B piece (Unit 2), and two 1" Fabric A squares to 5" Fabric B square (Unit 3). Press.

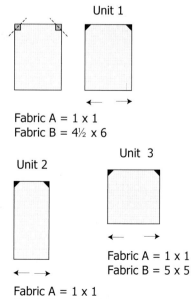

Unit 1

Fabric A = 1 x 1
Fabric B = 4½ x 6

Unit 2

Fabric A = 1 x 1
Fabric B = 3½ x 7

Unit 3

Fabric A = 1 x 1
Fabric B = 5 x 5

2. Sew one 1¼" x 3½" Fabric C piece between two 1" x 1¼" Fabric A pieces as shown. Press. Sew this unit to Unit 1 from step 1. Press. Sew one 3¼" x 4½" Fabric A piece to top of unit as shown. Press.

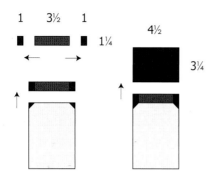

3. Sew one 1½" x 2½" Fabric C piece between two 1" x 1½" Fabric A pieces as shown. Press. Sew this unit to Unit 2 from step 1. Press. Sew one 3½" x 2" Fabric A piece to top of unit as shown. Press.

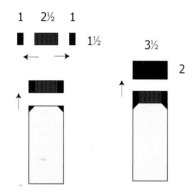

4. Sew one 1" x 4" Fabric C piece between two 1" Fabric A squares as shown. Press. Sew this unit to Unit 3 from step 1. Press. Sew one 4½" x 5" Fabric A piece to top of unit as shown. Press.

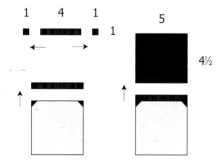

5. Sew units from step 2-4 together as shown. Press. Sew one 2½" x 12" Fabric D piece to bottom of unit. Press. Option: If desired, this piece can be made into a small quilt by simply adding borders, quilting, binding, and sewing decorative buttons to the jars.

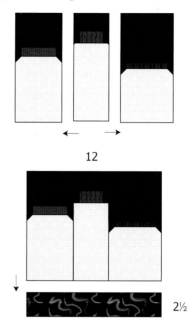

6. Sew unit from step 5 between two 2½" x 12" Fabric A pieces. Press seams toward Fabric A. Sew this unit between two 2½" x 15½" Fabric A strips as shown. Press.

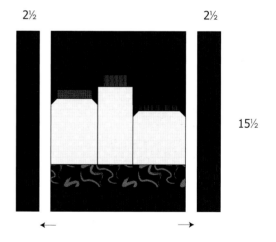

Assembling the Wall Art
The wall art uses a hinged shadow box and ⅛" foam core board. Our buttons were glued in place after the quilt was in the frame. If gluing is not desired, then sew buttons to quilt prior to wrapping and securing it around foam core board. Note: Sizes listed fit a 12" opening shadow box. If using a different size box, adjust size of strips and pieces as desired.

1. Place quilt top over 12" x 12" foam core board and center. Note: Make sure foam core fits into box opening. Adjust cut as needed. Pull fabric around to back and tape in middle of each side. Continue process, working from center out and stopping at corners. Pull corner tight and check front to make sure fabric is taut. Fold excess fabric at 90°, crease, and form corner. Tape in place. Repeat for all corners.

2. To make shelf covering, cut three ⅛" foam core boards to 2½" x 12". Stack foam core boards one on top of the other. Glue or tape together.

3. To make shelf covering fold 1" x 18½" Fabric F strip in half lengthwise wrong sides together and press. Baste to one long side of 1¼" x 18½" Fabric E strip matching raw edges. Sew unit between two 3½" x 18½" Fabric D strips as shown.

18½

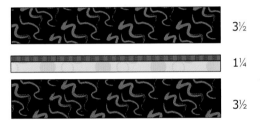

3½

1¼

3½

4. Cover shelf with unit from step 4, centering and aligning as needed. Tape excess to back of shelf.

5. Place wall art in shadow box and shelf on bottom front. Arrange decorative buttons on each jar. Once satisfied with arrangement, glue buttons in place. Display as desired.

NOTES FROM Debbie

One of my most sentimental books was called Collections From the Heart (1997) which was filled with projects featuring yo-yo, doily and button embellishments. One of the cutest projects was called Button...Button... and even included some Debbie Mumm buttons. The patchwork border dotted with buttons enhanced the old-fashioned style that was so popular at the time. I still have bins and jars full of buttons that I've collected over the years. These were a great resource from which I selected special buttons to include in this project.

What better way to update this than to modernize the colors, use black as the background, and set it all in a modern shadow box frame!

1997
Button...Button...
Originally featured in
Collections from
the Heart

General Directions

Cutting Strips and Pieces

We recommend washing cotton fabrics in cold water and pressing before making projects in this book. Using a rotary cutter, see-through ruler, and a cutting mat, cut the strips and pieces for the project. If indicated on the Cutting Chart, some will need to be cut again into smaller strips and pieces. Make second cuts in order shown to maximize use of fabric. The yardage amounts are based on an approximate fabric width of 42" and Fat Quarters are based on 18" x 22" pieces.

Pressing

Pressing is very important for accurate seam allowances. Press seams using either steam or dry heat with an "up and down" motion. Do not use side-to-side motion as this will distort the unit or block. Set the seam by pressing along the line of stitching, then press seams to one side as indicated by project instructions and diagram arrows.

Twisting Seams

When a block has several seams meeting in the center as shown, there will be less bulk if seam allowances are pressed in a circular type direction and the center intersection "twisted". Remove 1-2 stitches in the seam allowance to enable the center to twist and lay flat. This technique aids in quilt assembly by allowing the seams to fall opposite each other when repeated blocks are next to each other. The technique works well with 4-patch blocks, pinwheel blocks, and quarter-square triangle blocks.

Accurate Seam Allowance

Accurate seam allowances are always important, but especially when the blocks contain many pieces and the quilt top contains multiple pieced borders. If each seam is off as little as 1/16", you'll soon find yourself struggling with components that just won't fit.

To ensure seams are a perfect 1/4"-wide, try this simple test: Cut three strips of fabric, each exactly 1½" x 12". With right sides together, and long raw edges aligned, sew two strips together, carefully maintaining a 1/4" seam. Press seam to one side. Add the third strip to complete the strip set. Press and measure. The finished strip set should measure 3½" x 12". The center strip should measure 1"-wide, the two outside strips 1¼"-wide, and the seam allowances exactly 1/4".

If your measurements differ, check to make sure that seams have been pressed flat. If strip set still doesn't "measure up," try stitching a new strip set, adjusting the seam allowance until a perfect 1/4"-wide seam is achieved.

Assembly Line Method

Whenever possible, use an assembly line method. Position pieces right sides together and line up next to sewing machine. Stitch first unit together, then continue sewing others without breaking threads. When all units are sewn, clip threads to separate. Press seams in direction of arrows as shown in step-by-step project diagrams.

Quick Corner Triangles

Quick corner triangles are formed by simply sewing fabric squares to other squares or rectangles. The directions and diagrams with each project illustrate what size pieces to use and where to place squares on the corresponding piece. Follow steps 1–3 below to make quick corner triangle units.

1. With pencil and ruler, draw diagonal line on wrong side of fabric square that will form the triangle. This will be your sewing line.

   Sewing line

2. With right sides together, place square on corresponding piece. Matching raw edges, pin in place, and sew ON drawn line. Trim off excess fabric, leaving 1/4"-wide seam allowance as shown.

   Trim 1/4" away from sewing line

3. Press seam in direction of arrow as shown in step-by-step project diagram. Measure completed quick corner triangle unit to ensure the greatest accuracy.

   Finished quick corner triangle unit

Fussy Cut

To make a "fussy cut," carefully position ruler or template over a selected design in fabric. Include seam allowances before cutting desired pieces.

Quick-Fuse Appliqué

Quick-fuse appliqué is a method of adhering appliqué pieces to a background with fusible web. For quick and easy results, simply quick-fuse appliqué pieces in place. Use sewable, lightweight fusible web for the projects in this book unless otherwise indicated. Finish raw edges with stitching as desired. Laundering is not recommended unless edges are finished.

1. With paper side up, lay fusible web over appliqué pattern. Leaving ½" space between pieces, trace all elements of design. Cut around traced pieces, approximately ¼" outside traced line.

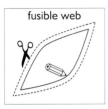

2. With paper side up, position and press fusible web to wrong side of selected fabrics. Follow manufacturer's directions for iron temperature and fusing time. Cut out each piece on traced line.

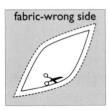

3. Remove paper backing from pieces. A thin film will remain on wrong side of fabric. Position and fuse all pieces of one appliqué design at a time onto background, referring to photos for placement. Fused design will be the reverse of traced pattern.

Appliqué Pressing Sheet

An appliqué pressing sheet is very helpful when there are many small elements to apply using a quick-fuse appliqué technique. The pressing sheet allows small items to be bonded together before applying them to the background. The sheet is coated with a special material that prevents fusible web from adhering permanently to the sheet. Follow manufacturer's directions. Remember to let fabric cool completely before lifting it from the appliqué sheet. If not cooled, the fusible web could remain on the sheet instead of on the fabric.

For accurate layout, place a line drawing of finished project under pressing sheet. Use this as a guide to adhere pieces.

Machine Appliqué

This technique should be used when you are planning to launder quick-fuse projects. Several different stitches can be used: small narrow zigzag stitch, satin stitch, blanket stitch, or another decorative machine stitch. Use an open toe appliqué foot if your machine has one. Use a stabilizer to obtain even stitches and help prevent puckering. Always practice first to check machine settings.

1. Fuse all pieces following Quick-Fuse Appliqué directions.

2. Cut a piece of stabilizer large enough to extend beyond the area to be stitched. Pin to the wrong side of fabric.

3. Select thread to match appliqué.

4. Following the order that appliqués were positioned, stitch along the edges of each section. Anchor beginning and ending stitches by tying off or stitching in place two or three times.

5. Complete all stitching, then remove stabilizer.

Hand Appliqué

Hand appliqué is easy when you start out with the right supplies. Cotton and machine embroidery thread are easy to work with. Pick a color that matches the appliqué fabric as closely as possible. Use appliqué or silk pins for holding shapes in place and a long, thin needle, such as a sharp, for stitching.

1. Make a template for every shape in the appliqué design. Use a dotted line to show where pieces overlap.

2. Place template on right side of appliqué fabric. Trace around template.

3. Cut out shapes ¼" beyond traced line.

4. Position shapes on background fabric, referring to quilt layout. Pin shapes in place.

5. When layering and stitching appliqué shapes, always work from background to foreground. Where shapes overlap, do not turn under and stitch edges of bottom pieces. Turn and stitch the edges of the piece on top.

6. Use the traced line as your turn-under guide. Entering from the wrong side of the appliqué shape, bring the needle up on the traced line. Using the tip of the needle, turn under the fabric along the traced line. Using blind stitch, stitch along folded edge to join the appliqué shape to the background fabric. Turn under and stitch about ¼" at a time.

Adding the Borders

1. Measure quilt through the center from side to side. Trim two border strips to this measurement. Sew to top and bottom of quilt. Press seams toward border.

2. Measure quilt through the center from top to bottom, including borders added in step 1. Trim border strips to this measurement. Sew to sides and press. Repeat to add additional borders.

Layering the Quilt

1. Cut backing and batting 4" to 8" larger than quilt top.

2. Lay pressed backing on bottom (right side down), batting in middle, and pressed quilt top (right side up) on top. Make sure everything is centered and that backing and batting are flat. Backing and batting will extend beyond quilt top.

3. Begin basting in center and work toward outside edges. Baste vertically and horizontally, forming a 3"–4" grid. Baste or pin completely around edge of quilt top. Quilt as desired. Remove basting.

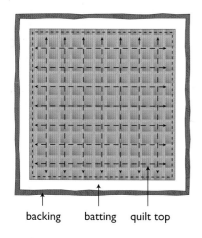

backing   batting   quilt top

Binding the Quilt

1. Trim batting and backing to ¼" beyond raw edge of quilt top. This will add fullness to binding.

2. Join binding strips to make one continuous strip if needed. To join, place 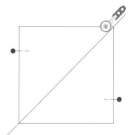 strips perpendicular to each other, right sides together, and draw a diagonal line. Sew on drawn line and trim triangle extensions, leaving a ¼"-wide seam allowance. Continue stitching ends together to make the desired length. Press seams open.

3. Fold and press binding strips in half lengthwise with wrong sides together.

4. Measure quilt through center from side to side. Cut two binding strips to this measurement. Lay binding strips on top and bottom edges of quilt top with raw edges of binding and quilt top aligned. Sew through all layers, ¼" from quilt edge. Press binding away from quilt top.

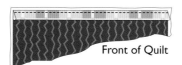

Front of Quilt

5. Measure quilt through center from top to bottom, including binding just added. Cut two binding strips to this measurement and sew to sides through all layers, including binding just added. Press.

6. Folding top and bottom first, fold binding around to back then repeat with sides. Press and pin in position. Hand-stitch binding in place using a blind stitch.

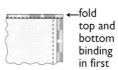

←fold top and bottom binding in first

Making Bias Strips

1. Refer to Fabric Requirements and Cutting Instructions for the amount of fabric required for the specific bias needed.

2. Remove selvages from the fabric piece and cut into a square. Mark edge with straight pin where selvages were removed as shown. Cut square once diagonally into two equal 45° triangles. (For larger squares, fold square in half diagonally and gently press fold. Open fabric square and cut on fold.)

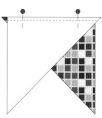

3. Place pinned edges right sides together and stitch along edge with a ¼" seam. Press seam open.

4. Using a ruler and rotary cutter, cut bias strips to width specified in quilt directions.

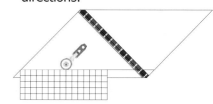

5. Each strip has a diagonal end. To join, place strips perpendicular to each other, right sides together, matching diagonal cut edges and allowing tips of angles to extend approximately ¼" beyond edges. Sew ¼"-wide seams. Continue stitching ends together to make the desired length. Press seams open. Cut strips into recommended lengths according to quilt directions.

Finishing Pillows

Any block in this book or combination of blocks can be made into an accent pillow. To determine the backing piece size needed, measure unfinished pillow top width and length. Divide the width measurement by two, and add 2¾" to this measurement. Cut two pieces of backing fabric to the new width measurement by the length measurement and follow directions below to complete pillow.

1. Layer batting between pillow top and lining. Baste. Hand or machine quilt as desired. Trim batting and lining even with raw edge of pillow top.
2. Narrow hem one long edge of each backing piece by folding under ¼" to wrong side. Press. Fold under ¼" again to wrong side. Press. Stitch along folded edge.
3. With sides up, lay one backing piece over second piece so hemmed edges overlap, making backing unit the same measurement as the pillow top. Baste backing pieces together at top and bottom where they overlap.

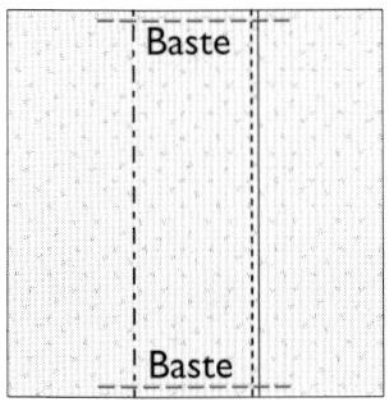

4. With right sides together, position and pin pillow top to backing. Using ¼"-wide seam, sew around edges, trim corners, turn right side out, and press.

Pillow Forms

Cut two pieces of fabric to size specified in project's materials needed list. Place right sides together, aligning raw edges. Using ¼"-wide seam, sew around all edges, leaving 5" opening for turning. Trim corners and turn right side out. Stuff to desired fullness with polyester fiberfill and hand-stitch opening closed.

Embroidery Stitch Guide

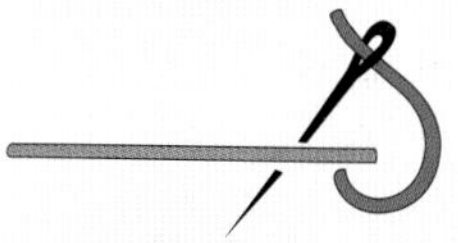

Anchored Straight Stitch

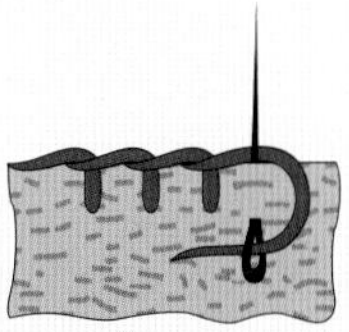

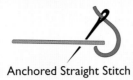

Blanket Stitch

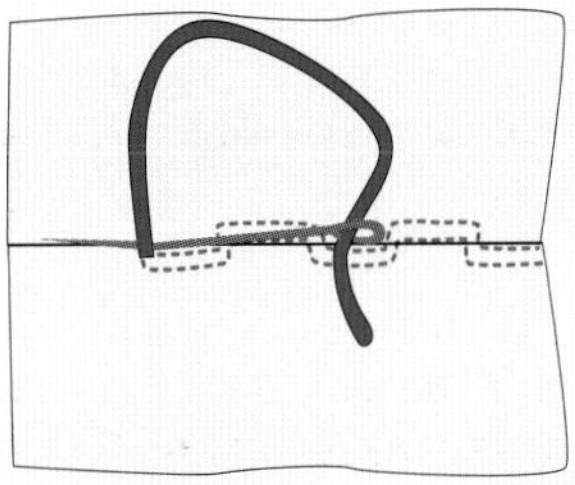

Blind Stitch

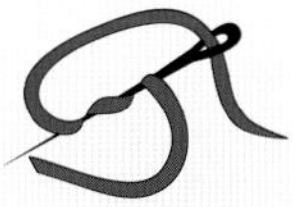

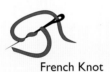

French Knot

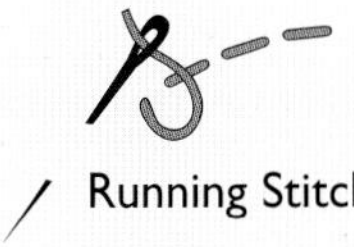

Running Stitch

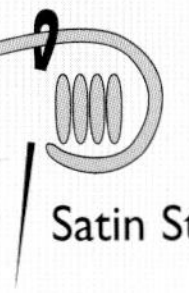

Satin Stitch

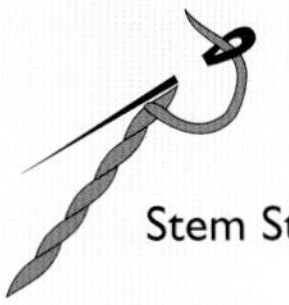

Stem Stitch

Metric Equivalency Chart

inches to mm			yds to meters	
inches	mm	cm	yards	meters
⅛	3	0.3	⅛	0.11
¼	6	0.6	⅙	0.15
½	13	1.3	¼	0.23
⅝	16	1.6	⅜	0.34
¾	19	1.9	½	0.46
⅞	22	2.2	⅝	0.57
1	25	2.5	¾	0.69
1¼	32	3.2	⅞	0.80
1½	38	3.8	1	0.91
1¾	44	4.4	1⅛	1.03
2	51	5.1	1¼	1.14
2½	64	6.4	1⅜	1.26
3	76	7.6	1½	1.37
3½	89	8.9	1⅝	1.49
4	102	10.2	1¾	1.60
4½	114	11.4	1⅞	1.71
5	127	12.7	2	1.83
6	152	15.2	2⅛	1.94
7	178	17.8	2¼	2.06
8	203	20.3	2⅜	2.17
9		22.9	2½	2.29
10	25.4		2⅝	2.40
12	30.5		2¾	2.51
13	33.0		2⅞	2.63
14	35.6		3	2.74
15	38.1		3⅛	2.86
16	40.6		3¼	2.97
17	43.2		3⅜	3.09
18	45.7		3½	3.20
19	48.3		3⅝	3.31
20	50.8		3¾	3.43
21	53.3		3⅞	3.54
22	55.9		4	3.66
23	58.4		4⅛	3.77
24	61.0		4¼	3.89
25	63.5		4⅜	4.00
26	66.0		4½	4.11
27	68.6		4⅝	4.23
28	71.1		4¾	4.34
29	73.7		4⅞	4.46
30	76.2		5	4.57
36	91.4		5⅛	4.69
42	106.7		5¼	4.80
			5⅜	4.91
			5½	5.03
			5⅝	5.14
			5¾	5.26
			5⅞	5.37
			6	5.49

1 meter = 39⅜"

A talented designer, author, and entrepreneur, Debbie Mumm has been creating charming artwork and quilt designs for twenty five years.

Debbie got her start in the quilting industry in 1986 with her unique and simple-to-construct quilt patterns. Since that time, she has authored more than sixty books featuring quilting and home decorating projects and has led her business to become a multi-faceted enterprise that includes publishing, fabric design, and licensed art divisions.

Known world-wide for the many licensed products that feature her designs, Debbie loves to bring traditional elements together with fresh palettes and modern themes to create the look of today's country.

Designs by Debbie Mumm

Special thanks to my creative teams:

Editorial & Project Design

Debbie Mumm: Managing Editor & Designer
Carolyn Ogden: Editor
Nancy Kirkland: Quilt Designer/Seamstress
Georgie Gerl: Technical Writer/Editor
Anita Pederson: Machine Quilter

Book Design & Production

Monica Ziegler: Graphic Designer

Photography

Tom Harlow
Carolyn Ogden: Photo Stylist
Debbie Mumm: Photo Stylist

Art Team

Kathy Arbuckle: Artist/Designer • Gil-Jin Foster: Artist
Jackie Saling: Designer

Special thanks to Nick and Carolyn Ogden for opening their home for photography.
The Debbie Mumm® Sewing Studio exclusively uses Bernina® sewing machines.

Library of Congress Control Number: 2011927987

Produced by:

Debbie Mumm, Inc.
1015 N Calispel Street
Suite A
Spokane, WA 99201
(509) 466-3572
Fax (509) 466-6919

www.debbiemumm.com

Discover More from Debbie Mumm®

Fresh Cuts
by Debbie Mumm®

112-page, soft cover

Debbie Mumm's®
Quick Quilts for Home

112-page, soft cover

Debbie Mumm's®
I Care with Quilts

96-page, soft cover

Debbie Mumm's®
HomeComings

96-page, soft cover

Published by:

Leisure Arts, Inc
5701 Ranch Drive
Little Rock, AR · 72223
www.leisurearts.com

Available at local fabr
and craft shops or a
debbiemumm.com